UNEG

Love

MALCOLM CHERRY

Ordering Information:

Prime Seven Media
518 Landmann St.
Tomah City, WI 54660

Printed in the United States of America

TABLE OF CONTENTS

Chapter 1   Time to Say Goodbye............................ 11

Chapter 2   The Mist of Time.................................. 22

Chapter 3   The Birth of Anne-Marie.................... 32

Chapter 4   Home at Last.. 48

Chapter 5   Dash to Gt. Yarmouth General

                       Hospital 57

Chapter 6   The Search for A Cause........................ 86

Chapter 7   Taking Amanda Home....................... 102

Chapter 8   Ignorance at Its Worst.........................111

Chapter 9   Started another New Drug................ 122

Chapter 10   At Long Last Great Ormond

                       Street Hospital 136

Chapter 11   The Day of The Conference 156

Chapter 12   The Lonely Journey Home 163

Chapter 13   Return to Great Ormond Street....... 168

Chapter 14   Amanda's Placed in an

                       Induced Coma 176

Chapter 15   Transfer Back to Gt. Yarmouth........ 189

Chapter 16   We Believe in Miracles 195

Chapter 17   Dreams Can Come True..................... 214

Chapter 18   Wind of Change 222

Chapter 19   Happy First Birthday Amanda..........230

Chapter 20   Visit from Social Workers..................236

Chapter 21   Happy Third Birthday Amanda........248

Chapter 22   Moving Home......................................260

Chapter 23   Starting School....................................270

Chapter 24   A Change of Amanda's

             Paediatrician...284

Chapter 25   A Major Opperation 315

Chapter 26   Goodnight Sweetheart Goodnight...334

Chapter 27   The Final Chapter 340

PROLOGUE

My name is Malcolm Cherry. There are many personal stories I could tell were it not for the fact I had made a promise to write this story as it unfolded, a story that has neither a beginning nor an ending, a true story about a special little girl by the name of "Amanda-Louise Cherry; "Whose life was dramatically cut short by an unknown medical issue."

For almost thirty years I have struggled to put into words, the full effect it has had on family members; and which seriously continues unbelievably to this day. Questions which still haunt us even now, answers around serious errors and delays created by hospital administrators. They did not pick up or notice the growing number of failures, failures that had either been missed or ignored by the Paediatrician we thought we had confidently placed Amanda's care and safety too.

Failure after failure not being able to listen to other opinion both medical and more concerning taking a seemingly laidback attitude regarding the passing critical information to medical staff from some hospital departments, their lack of speed with which any results were being fed down. In my humble opinion it did in some way contribute in missed opportunities by paediatricians desperately trying to diagnose some form of medical prognosis. Every second of every day, I find myself reliving the daily torments which remain deeply engraved in my mind to this day. It is as a distraught grieving father that I sit here painfully putting pen to paper.

The feeling of deep crushing disappointment by those reaching out for the same answers to Amanda's demise, as we her parents are searching desperately for. The relentless anger I feel continues to dwell deep and festering inside, adding to the slow and wilful destruction of mind body and soul. A story about a special little girl by the name of "Amanda-Louise Cherry, we owe our personal thanks to the support that was given by the many close valid friends and family members, who were there in our hours of need unaware how much their help reduced much of the pain we all felt.

We will never forget them; all will remain in our hearts eternally…. "Thank you"!

[I am fully aware of the legal matters regarding the use of real people's names, so, I would like to formally declare that the names of many characters within this story bear no resemblance intentionally or otherwise to persons either living or dead.] [Except Amanda's GP's and Professor Doctor Back.]

ACKNOWLEDGEMENTS

We would like to offer our deep sincere personal and affectionate thanks to family and friends for all their support commitment and understanding given to Amanda Louise throughout her short fragile life.

WE SHALL NEVER FORGET YOU!

Mum & Dad Hazelwood, Mr. & Mrs. Borrett, Mr. & Mrs Carter, Mr. Collins, Mrs. Smith. Mr. & Mrs Ford, Mrs. Gould, Mr. Holman, Mrs. Shaw, Mr. & Mrs. Collyier, Mrs. Eaton. Mrs. Twinehall, Mrs. Ryder, Mrs. Harper, Mrs. Ayers, Mrs. Dell, Mrs. Pearson, Mr. & Mrs, Jones, Mrs. Westcott, Rose-Marie Dunelian, Mrs. Scoot, Mr & Mrs. Runacres, Mr. Wilson, Mr & Mrs Field, Mr. & Mrs. Rackham, Mrs. Watts, Mrs Ford, Mrs. Clappison Mrs. Durant (Suffolk County Council), (UK Prime Minister Mrs. Margaret Thatcher), Mr. David Porter MP). Mrs. Woodcock, Mrs. & Mrs. Carter (Suffolk County

Council), Mr. & Mrs. Cushion, Doctor Mower, Doctor Dutter, Doctor Van Pelt, Doctor Kelly, Doctor Anderson, Doctor Markham, Doctor Livingstone, Mrs Gillian Anderson, Sister Penny Yates, Mrs. Allington-Smith, Close family friends Mick & Jo (Yvonne's mum and Dads next door neighbours of many years), Mrs. Jervis, The Reverend William Stewart.

There is one group who will always remain deep in our hearts, often or never given a second thought. If it were not for them Amanda would not have survived to the age of Ten, Doctors & Nursing Staff of Gt. Yarmouth Hospital Children's Ward. Doctors & Nursing Staff of Lowestoft's Hospital Children's Ward.

Doctors & Nursing Staff of the James Paget Hospital Gorleston. Doctors & Nursing Staff of Great Ormand Street Hospital for Sick Children London (GOSH).

A CHILD
OF
CHRIST

1990

THIS IS A TRUE STORY

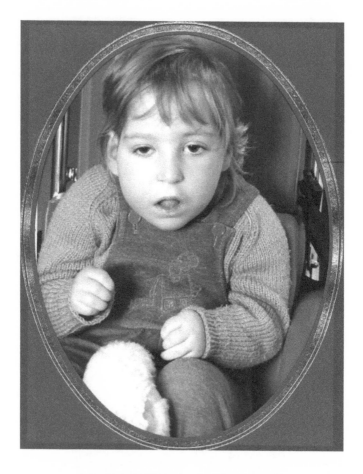

AMANDA LOUISE
1979 – 1990

THIS BOOK IS DEDICATED
TO THE MEMORY OF OUR
DEAR BELOVED DAUGHTER
AMANDA LOUISE CHERRY

Age Ten Years and Six Months

Born Wednesday 19th. September 1979

At the Northgate Hospital Gt. Yarmouth.

Fell Asleep Sunday 4th. March 1990

In the Children's Ward

Of the James Paget Hospital

Gt. Yarmouth

At 21:10 Hours

R.I.P.

Chapter One

TIME TO
SAY GOODBYE

Time passes all too quickly in this life, it seems like only yesterday we were preparing for the arrival of our second child Amanda Louise. Now as the sound of distant bells slowly fades; two large Black funeral cars come to a gentle halt in front of our bungalow. There in the rear of a hearse lay a small white casket: it is covered in floral tributes, small brass handles, glisten blindly as they were totally engulfed by the clear bright morning sunlight.

The time is 11 a.m. Monday 12th March 1990, the sky is deep blue, the air so crisp and cool one's breath can be seen quite clearly. We are now about to say our final goodbyes, for at precisely 11.30am at Gt. Yarmouth Crematorium in Gorleston, where the funeral of our daughter Amanda Louise Cherry will take place.

As if time were an issue; the funeral director guided us into the Car behind. Amanda's sister Anne-Marie taking the first place. She is 17 years old and almost 6 foot tall. She has shoulder length hair brown eyes and found it quite a problem trying to climb into the car as she was 7 months pregnant with her first child. The baby is due on or about the 19th. of May 1990, it is hard to imagine the stress being placed on both Anne-Marie and the baby but her strength of character will, I am convinced show through.

As parents both Yvonne and I have a great deal of pride in the way Anne- Marie has managed to cope not only with her sister's illness over the last 10 years, but more importantly in the way she has managed Amanda's eventual passing. The trauma of losing a sister is something we shall both have in common for the rest of our Lives, when at the age of ten I too lost my sister Christine who at the tender age of 8, passed away painfully suffering a Brain tumour.

My mother was next to take her seat in the car, she is a well-built woman in her sixties, with jet black curly hair. Looking at her you would be forgiven if you believed she was only in her fifty's: she was born in Germany a smallish town named Gottingen, a great deal of her life as a child had been spent in an orphanage. At the age of 15yrs she met and fell in love with a handsome young Englishman serving in Her Majesty's Armed Forces. After what can only be described as a whirlwind courtship, they both married, unfortunately? this was doomed not to last, and as the saying goes that is another story.

Following closely behind was my stepfather Alex my, a quiet and somewhat shy person. He is about five foot ten inches and at least eleven stone in weight and at times is prone to be the battering ram from mother's verbal attacks. Saying that; I must point out that Alex is no wimp, he has always been there for her. Alex is I would say her knight in shining armour and wanted for nothing, those are my mother's words not mine.

Yvonne's mother who also is in her sixtieth year made her way slowly toward the car, a proud, upstanding woman in every sense of the word. She stopped briefly for a moment before the hearse looking at Amanda's casket, with tears in her eyes, I watched as she mouthed a short prayer. Like my mother, she too has been blessed with a youthful look. I am convinced the youthfulness of both these women are due to their active lifestyles and Gods Intervention in the book of life.

Yvonne's father unfortunately had to sit next to the driver in the car; he is a short well-dressed man in his sixties with thinning grey hair, sadly he has not been lucky with a youthful look. Yvonne's dad sadly suffers nerves or at least has done ever since I have had the pleasure of knowing him.

There were now only two places left in the back of the car, these were going to be taken by Yvonne and me. We were the last to take our place in the car only to pause momentarily as we were forced to look at a small white casket surrounded by floral tributes of assorted sizes, I remember thinking this was a bad nightmarish dream, pleading for answers; asking God, "Please God" what has gone wrong with this mad crazy world we live in"? For is the first time in my Christian life, I can say in all honesty; that "YES" I was expecting an Answer but none were forthcoming.

Yvonne a slender woman of 39 years; deep brown hair brown eyes and intellectually bright. She has managed to find strength to manage this traumatic experience, I am not sure how long it will be before she too will capitulate too the reality of what has happened. As we sat stiffly on the rear seats, we clung tightly to each other in hope of finding comfort. This was increasing made difficult with every turn of the car's wheels, as there looking back at us were two exceptionally large brown glistening eyes of a large pink floral Teddy Bear holding a pink rose in its paw staring relentlessly back at us through the rear window of the leading hears.

Before beginning the short twenty-minute journey to the Crematorium at Gorleston, the funeral director approached Amanda's casket as if hinged at the hip he respectfully and what seemed, like ages ceremoniously bowed toward her. He then stood bolt upright, turned sharply to his right and drew his heels together with a sharp 'crack'! He then marched to the head of the procession and continued to walk slowly for about one hundred yards, with the procession of cars following slowly behind then. Then without stopping he managed in one movement to open the lead cars front door climbed in and we continued to the funeral.

No one can fully describe the pain and heartache felt watching a loved one Albeit the lifeless body of someone who a few weeks ago were living and breathing, and now lying in a coffin. We are forced to watch as Amanda's tiny white casket, makes its final journey down to a Crematorium oven, or watch as the final curtain closes at the end of a Cremation Service life Can prove to be so cruel. We now are permanently separated from all we have held so dear.

Yet regrettably we all face this traumatic moment in our short fragile and precious earthly lives, no matter how painful it may or may not be. For Yvonne and me it was a feeling of numbness, of being in a black empty void everything seemed so far away, the sense of loneliness filled our very being. Sound appears muffled unreal, inwardly our cries for help to waken us from this nightmare is never heard. A weird sense of drowning engulfs our whole body. Our mind screams out in hope someone will soon wake us, to find it was all just a bad dream.

Finally, Anne-Marie's Partner Denis was the last to appear from the bungalow, he is a smart well-dressed shy young man of 25 years and about 5 foot 6 inches tall. He has cropped short fair hair although

Anne-Marie assures me it is ginger. Denis decided that he would drive to the funeral himself, he would take those who had no transport and wish to go?

This young man has clearly proved too be a tower of strength for Anne-Marie, his loyalty and support are going to be evaluated to the limit over the next few months. Heads are filled full of questions, questions which will frustratingly never receive an answer no matter how long or hard you try believe me I know, I'm still trying to this day.

The service was over all too quickly, and now it was final. All we had left were our precious memories, no matter how much we loved Amanda we were forced to let her go. That for us really is proving the hardest thing. Strange as it may seem, after the service, both Yvonne and I became aware of Amanda's presence: we both were experiencing a feeling of comfort, peace, and yes, even a feeling of tranquillity. At that moment we knew Amanda was finally at peace, the pain and suffering she had been put through in all her short life had now been taken away.

It became evidently clear just how Amanda had touched many people's lives during her brief time with us. There were many nurses from the James Paget and Lowestoft's children's wards who over the years have in one way or another become overly attached to her. Many teachers who we had a very close-knit bond took time off from the Warren Special School in Beccles Road where Amanda was a pupil to say their own final good-byes, the biggest surprise came from the many relatives not seen for so many years. many having travelled from far flung places across England Scotland, Wales, Yorkshire, and Liverpool just to name a few so they could say in their own way: "Good-bye Amanda, and God Bless!"

Sadly, we were unable to speak at any length with most of those who came, as they needed to return home again as soon as the service had ended. There was not a single dry eye, as each person in turn gave us a few words of comfort, everyone repeated the same thing. That "Amanda's passing has left a large gap in their lives that would never be filled, clearly, she would always be greatly missed."

I became annoyingly aware the fact the drivers of funeral cortege were beginning to become agitated and eager to return to Lowestoft, they were restlessly walking up and down impatiently holding open the car doors, with a great deal of reluctance we began to edge us toward the car pausing and looking back. Yvonne and I were desperately hoping Amanda would dash through the chapel doors and straight into our arms, of course that was not going to happen.

As we passed through the main gates the emotional strain began to ware us both down. Many mourners came back to the bungalow; it was a chance to have a family catch up but more to the point the ability to remember all the happy times we had, nothing lasts forever and as the day progressed those who had travelled some distance had to make their way home, we had the chance to thank each one of them in person for coming before they left.

Eventually only our parents remained, and in a way, we were rather pleased, we wanted to return to the Crematorium to have a better look at the flowers sent for Amanda, we were so emotionally stressed after the service we had no chance to really see them.

The Cemetery and Crematorium closes about 7 pm or as they say dusk, so, we did not have much time. We drove round to the side of the chapel to find the flowers had been placed outside, and the chapel doors were firmly closed.

The atmosphere was so peaceful and tranquil there, we forgot it was time to go home. On our return the bungalow was incredibly quiet, and, in many ways, it felt rather strange, as I sat next to Amanda's empty chair in the corner of the living room, I was aware of a flickering light bulb above my head suddenly, without warning there was a loud "POP!" as the bulb blew. it was rather strange because we have never had a problem with that light bulb in all the years, we have lived here.

Was Amanda trying to let us know that even though her life with us was finally over, she would now remain with us in a spiritual form. The day had been a long traumatic one for us all and tomorrow was not going to be any easier, my mother and Alex must return home. For them, the long journey to Harrogate will be long and sad, although they do plan to return later for the birth of Anne-Marie's baby. The strain of the day proved too much for me, and by the early evening, I seriously broke down.

Yvonne had no alternative but to call the doctor who was knocking on the door within 15 minutes. After giving me a thorough examination, he asked if I had been taking my medication, I told him that I had not, and I really could not care less, the only thing I wanted at this very moment was to be with Amanda. Concerned by my response I was given a strong talking to by the doctor, he at once increased the amount of medication I was also taking an antidepressant a sleeping drug which in about 20 minutes were starting to work. After an exceptionally long and tiring day and the fact the sedative I had been given we decided an early night would be of some benefit, there were still many more plans that needed attention but would have to wait till tomorrow.

Even though the sedatives did their job, Yvonne and I were up with the lark as usual. Well, how do you break ten years of sleeping lightly listening out for Amanda.

Chapter Two

THE MIST
OF TIME

We slept well, all things considering, but today is going to be rather hectic. Amanda's ashes should hopefully arrive at Rivets funeral Services sometime today, although no specific time has been given. Marion Small, a close and valid friend of ours works as a Secretary for Rivets funeral Services, she is an extremely attractive woman in her early 40's about 5 foot 8 tall, with short dark hair and slender build. Her soft speaking voice gives an ambient calmness to those she speaks too and ideally embellished the job she has.

I have personally known Marion for several years we were both members of the Quaysides amateur dramatics Society that's naturally another story which I spoke of earlier. We were all up with the lark this morning not that we could sleep much anyway, nervously awaiting the telephone call informing us that Rivets had received Amanda's ashes, also mum and Alex were today returning home to Harrogate something Yvonne and I were not relishing.

At approximately 3 pm we received the expected telephone call from Marion, she informed us that Amanda's ashes had arrived. She also confirmed those arrangements had been made for the internment of Amanda's ashes, this would take place at 2 pm on Friday afternoon at the Kirkley Cemetery. The Reverend William Stewart who knows Amanda personally has agreed to officiate at the service. The decision to have the internment so soon was not an easy one, but we felt that to prolong it would cause more grief than was necessary. Friday morning was soon upon us, and it was a glorious day, the sun was shining, and it was quite warm. We cannot get over the way the weather has been on two of the four worse days in our lives, did not help to improve the way we were feeling.

Monday the 12th of March for her funeral and today Friday March the 16th for the internment service. It was as if Amanda was trying to tell us something. I really do not know! Maybe it was conformation in respect we should be happy not sad, she was as free as a bird so to speak, no longer a prisoner trapped inside a useless body, running, and jumping seeing with her own eyes the real beauty of her surroundings and finally having a wonderful time.

All these God given gifts we mere mortals take for granted; and Amanda has now for the first time been given a chance to experience them for herself. If this is the case; all we can say my darling is, "Enjoy Every Wonderful Moment!" We arrived at the Cemetery at two o'clock, as we got out of our car, we were approached by the funeral director who was carrying a small brown urn. On the lid in small white letters was the inscription 'Amanda Louise Cherry.' "Died 4th March 1990." "Aged 10 years."

This small little urn was all that was left of our beloved daughter, now that too was being taken from us and her final resting place was here in the "Kirkley Cemetery." As we approached the graveside, a hole no bigger than 8 inches by 8 inches and 3 feet deep slowly the funeral director knelt and gently placed Amanda's urn at the bottom of the grave.

Emotions took over again as Reverend William Stewart said a small prayer for the internment of Amanda's ashes, once again the emotions were the same as the we had at her funeral and the night she passed in the Hospital crying holding on to each other trying to come to terms with everything all over again. As if nothing else could further torment us when suddenly from out of nowhere. appeared a council Cemetery worker he was so quick no ounce of respect or compassion was shown from him; with a shovel in hand, he began to cover Amanda's urn, "What was the hurry" she was not going anywhere?" It felt to us almost like he wanted to be somewhere other than here.

Anyway, we hardly had time to say goodbye as he filled in the grave, arrangements had been made for a marble plaque to be placed over the grave, unfortunately, we were informed that apparently before any that could be done the land must be allowed to settle for at least a couple of days. now we must wait.

Naturally, I was fearful of losing Amanda's exact place, so, to make sure, this would not happen I found a large twig and embedded it in the exact spot. "Large Twig!" said Yvonne, "more like half a tree if you ask me!" at least we were able to crack a little joke.

The hours and days pass slowly for us now, both Yvonne and I are finding it hard adjusting to the fact, we no longer must follow a daily routine. There were times when we would be working well into the early hours, especially if Amanda was ill

Jobs that needed to be done are too many to list, but all were important to her wellbeing. It is now almost three weeks since Amanda's passing, the pain is still as unbearable as that last night in Hospital. It was made worse today as we remove the 101 sympathy cards from the surrounding walls

and doors placing them in a special album in hope it will ease the pain, but only time will tell. Great news today the headstone has been laid and now we have a marker for Amanda.

It is beautifully made white satin marble with an Angel placed at the top right corner a tear on her cheek being wiped away, the inscription is done in black writing and reads:

In Loving Memory
Of our
Darling Daughter
Amanda Louise Cherry
Who Fell Asleep
4th March 1990 Aged 10 yrs
Till We Meet Again

No matter how much I try, I cannot lose this guilt I have, the guilt that in some way it was my fault Amanda's life had been ended at such an early age. For years I have been asking that Amanda has a much-needed hip operation, and for just as long I had been told that she would not survive it by every doctor I asked; but still I kept on pushing; and pushing.

Eventually all the pushing did pay off; "if only I had left things alone"! Why did I not listen? If I had done so, then Amanda would still be alive. This is the pain and guilt I must endure and will stay with me to my final resting place, I feel that my constant pushing clearly to try to reduce Amanda's pain had dramatically Contributed to Amanda's demise as surely as if I had placed a gun to her head and squeezed the trigger. I pray she will forgive me for all the pain and suffering I had put her through in the short life she had on this earth, I really thought I was doing the best for her, boy, was I so, so very wrong.

Now the cost of getting it so wrong her ashes lay in a cold and bleak Cemetery as an eternal reminder to my own stupidity. I am not sure how long I shall be able to continue before I finally snap at this moment my bottle of anti-depressant tablets are looking very inviting to me. Every moment of the day all I can see is Amanda's face, the only time I have any peace is when I visit her grave and beg for forgiveness. As I stand looking down at a small bunch of flowers that at this moment mark Amanda's grave, tears are running down my face.

Strangely I felt very cold; a musky smell like that of boiling nappies so strong I can even taste it in my throat. I cannot explain that strange cold feeling that spread through my body as if someone had; excuse the pun walked over my grave; it caused me to shiver and I felt a little apprehensive and slightly frightened; but at the same time a quiet peace and stillness.

I was aware someone was standing next to me holding my hand and I hear a soft gentle voice of a little girl, yet as I physically turned and looked, I could not see anyone, now my mind went into hyper drive what was happening this certainly is a no joking matter, to officially announce that I can hear a voice as plain as day speaking and clearly is certainly not wise or helpful in our current climate. I was aware of a dampish mist starting to build up around me, a small hand gently taking hold of mine and what sounded like the voice of a young child speaking to me softly, reassuring me not to worry and that all is well.

I am unable to say who was speaking only to say it was an incredibly young girl's voice, it was also accompanied by; how I can explain it? a sense of being wrapped or engulfed in a deep fluffy warm blanket, "yes!" I would say that is the closes thing to that feeling. I find myself starting to relive our lives over again like "Ground Hog Day or Charles Dickins Scrouge in a Christmas Carol" or Was too about to die? It is said that your life flashes by you, yet I was in no pain but strange as it may seem I was immersed in a warm glow and being unbelievably comforted as I said by the soft gentle voice of a little girl as she gently held my hand.

Yvonne and I started our family exceedingly early on in our marriage in fact it was only around nine months or so, how surprised we were as Yvonne joyfully announced she was pregnant with Anne-Marie. It proved to be a problem pregnancy for me, I was fine up till the last 8 days of her pregnancy it was very painful. I have never in my whole life experienced stomach cramps so strong.

I was visiting the first aid department of the Birdseye factory in Lowestoft every hour for something to help with the pain, I did not want to throw up, but it was just the relentless pain and informed that my face had become quite a pale colour. A colleague at work who also needed to see the nurse was laughing her head off, personally, I could see what was so grippingly funny, this was certainly no laughing matter and I felt quite angry. She informed the nurse that my wife was pregnant and nearing the end of her term, the diagnosis; I was suffering labour pains and was told to go home and now both were finding it humorously funny. It's going to be all round the shop floor in 10 minutes or so.

The weekend was almost upon us, and I was to see how I felt on Monday as I was working 12-hour night shift (6 pm till 6 am) this is the best shift to be rostered on the management tended to let you get on with your work only showing themselves if there was a fundamental problem that stopped the machines from running. The labour pains had dramatically rescinded thank heaven but the thought of them starting again, made me quite anxious, followed by the desperate struggle for seven long years to conceive another child.

Eventually the feeling of over-whelming joy, as we were informed that Yvonne was finally pregnant after having at least 4 miscarriages. Now just 10 years and 6 months ago, Amanda was born. Little did we know how much she would touch our lives, and those who were to privilege enough to nurse her over the years.

Chapter Three

THE BIRTH OF ANNE-MARIE

hen Yvonne fell pregnant with our first child. It was a fantastic feeling; we were so excited we could hardly wait for the birth of our little one. Yvonne made it quite; quite clear at the outset, she wanted to have a home birth something the midwife tried to discourage in case God forbid should any complications arise and there was a need to get to hospital. Yvonne was adamant a home birth is what she wanted, and a home birth she would have.

As the birth date drew nearer, I had a feeling Yvonne was becoming rather apprehensive. Is not strange that with all the available medical aid, including books or diagrams in all the world, nothing can ever come close to explaining or preparing a woman for the pain she must undergo during childbirth.

Yvonne was in labour for only a brief time, or at least that's what it seemed like. By 3.30 am on Friday morning 11th of February 1972, I stood transfixed, as I watched the most wonderful sight in the world. Yvonne had hold of my hand and the strength of her grip was likened to a bench vice, "one more push" cried the Midwife not to be outdone I turned to Yvonne and cried out "OK one more push darling."

Yvonne shouted out "Ah shut up!" then landed a right-hook punch to the side of my face. It was well worth the right hander as out popped our first child, and "It was a Girl." She weighed in at a staggering 8 pounds 14 ounces, a right little bruiser. We decided there and then; to name her Anne-Marie and boy did she have a set of lungs on her and would certainly out match any town crier in the land. When Anne-Marie was 9 months old, we decided time was right to try for another baby, but alas as most people know when you try planning something "Sod's Law" will inevitably step in and prevent those plans from reaching fruition.

This proved to be one of those occasions, it took almost 7 months for Yvonne to fall pregnant again. Sadly, 12 weeks into the pregnancy she aborted, many tears were naturally shed, for a woman especially this is emotionally upsetting and the fact her gynaecologist was either unable or refused to tell us why. That traumatic experience inevitably took its toll on Yvonne, as she blamed herself for this loss what had she done; or not done to account for this outcome? Sadly, this would prove not to be an isolated event, as it again, happened 3 more times.

The traumatic experience was taking its toll on me but more so, with Yvonne so we decided that we would reluctantly place a hold on our trying. Instead, we would try and discover the reasons why she continually did not take her pregnancies to full term. Yvonne felt she was an inadequate mother, for a long time having to contend with the pressures of trying to fall pregnant again, was the last thing on her mind. Yvonne also had to struggle when her friends visited with their new-born babies and felt reluctant to hold any of them. I really felt for Yvonne the pain could plainly be seen in her eyes the painful battle she was having with her emotions, she desperately wanted to cuddle their babies I was lost for what to do unfortunately I was too inadequate to understand how I could successfully comfort her.

As time went on; the support from family and friends paid off, we found ourselves expectant parents. Hopes of having another child were again just pipe dreams, as two months into the pregnancy a problem arose, and Yvonne lost this one too. I became fearful that this loss would severely affect Yvonne she would end up worse than before, but this was not the case; instead, she desperately wanted answers. "Where did we go wrong?" For four years we continued trying for a child, we were so desperate to have another baby that we were prepared to do anything.

Over the next few weeks, we underwent many blood tests, sperm counts, and egg counts. Anyone who has been through this will know the dilemma we faced for me, the job of trying to make love to a specimen bottle was not only degrading and almost impossible, but most of all it was sole destroying and embarrassing. No one was left in any doubt as to what you we're being asked to do, when in full view of other patients waiting to be seen by a doctor, a nurse hands you a brown paper bag and a Pornographic magazine; then tells you that the toilets are outside and to the left of the building.

We were told the results of the tests would be ready in about 2 weeks, and an appointment would be sent for us to see the Dr. The awaited phone call arrives 8 days later, and we were asked to attend the Lowestoft hospitals fertility clinic for a 1.30 pm appointment to be given the test results. All our fears about those results were for nothing; the test results came back with flying colours, Yvonne was producing an exceptionally high number of eggs and as for me, my sperm production was exorbitantly high so why are we having problems? Eventually medical help was given, and over the next few months Yvonne's ordeal of taking daily temperature readings and keeping a record of her oestrogen levels. After about 3 months, she was placed on a fertility drug called 'Clomid'. This drug according to her doctor should improve her chances of falling pregnant. Now after almost 7 years of physical pain, tears and doubt, Yvonne is again I am over the moon to say finally Yvonne is pregnant with our second child I am convinced that her gynaecologist will be keeping an awfully close watch on her progress because of the past problems.

As I lay staring up at the bedroom ceiling there was a noticeable sound of nothingness, not a twittering bird or passing car could be heard only the ticking of the alarm clocks second hand surprisingly, hypnotic sound broke the peace and tranquillity in the room. Suddenly the alarm clock rang it sounded almost like a fire bell, I slammed my hand on the stop button and laid there for a snooze it was only four thirty on a cold dark Tuesday morning in September and did not have to be in work till 6 am. I had been unable to sleep well throughout the night and had been suffering from severe stomach cramps.

Yvonne suddenly dug her elbow into the small of my back, "Come on" she said. "it's time you got up; otherwise, you're going to be late for work." I angrily snapped back at her. "Oh, for God's sake." Reluctantly I crawl out of bed, after doing the necessaries, I took a couple of tablets to try and ease the stomach pain I had. Even after taking 2 paracetamol tablets the nagging pain remained with me all morning. I spent a great deal of time travelling to and from the companies first aid department. It was while on my 5th visit, a young girl asked if Yvonne had given birth to her baby yet.

Now that explains everything" said the duty sister. I was, in her words not mine "Suffering from sympathy Labour Pains." I was both pleased and embarrassed, at the same time, I'm sure it showed on my face. I really thought I had eaten something which had disagreed with me but could not for the life of me think what. Still knowing that the pain was not improving, in fact it felt as if it were increasing in intensity "So nothing too serious then" I snapped. Nonetheless for me it was rather embarrassing, the nurse gave me a tablet and said, "go home poor man," with a large smirk on her face "I will call your department supervisor and let him know.

Yvonne has been having contractions all day but with no pain I'm not surprised because I was suffering each one and it was not a laughing matter, "it was like lesser amounts of pressure across my stomach and back" she said. By teatime, the duration of each contraction was between 2 and 3 minutes, but the pain I was having seemed to last for ever. Enough is Enough I decided to telephone the maternity unit at Gt. Yarmouth's Northgate Hospital, I asked to be put through to the duty doctor but instead ended up with the Maternity ward sister. After explaining the situation fully to her, I asked if I should bring my wife over to be checked by the doctor. "By all means you can bring your wife over Mr Cherry" she firmly said. "But she must be admitted first." By 7.30 pm in the evening the contractions had become stronger, although the spacing between each had not changed. I become rather worried as for some strange reason I was no longer having any pain, "Why?" I felt it might be prudent to take Yvonne to the hospital. On arrival Yvonne was taken onto the maternity ward and I was made to wait outside, it must have been a good hour before the ward sister returned to see me.

Yvonne was comfortable and in bed, I was recommended to go home and telephone hourly for updates on her progress. I asked if I would be allowed to say good night, but this was refused and insisted I leave at once. Naturally, I was upset and angry at being spoken to like that as I turned to leave, I think I mumbled "Nasty little woman" or words to that effect but not too sure if she had heard as she cleared her thought quite loudly...To get my own back for not being allowed to say good night.

I took the instruction of telephoning every hour to the letter. I hardly slept a wink all night, it seemed an eternity for the sun to rise. By 8 pm there was still no news from the hospital, like many expectant fathers I was gradually becoming more and more impatient. Following orders from the ward sister, I telephoned to find out how Yvonne had been over night and what the position was with regards to an imminent birth. I was informed Yvonne had slept well and that the Doctor was with her. Also, Yvonne had been placed on an Intravenous Drip (I.V.), to help induce labour, I was assured by the ward sister that there was no need for concern and that she would have me called as soon as it were necessary. I hardly had time to replace the receiver and walk away from the telephone when it rang again. "Mr Cherry!" can you get over to the hospital as soon as possible please? your wife has just been taken into the delivery room. At that moment, my mind went into over-drive: the adrenaline being pumped round my body caused me to panic. It took me less than half an hour to reach the hospital, I must have broken every speed limit known to humankind.

On entering the Maternity Department, I reported to the receptionist, who informed the medical staff of my arrival, I did not have to wait long. Heading toward me at great speed were two well-built nurses, each with their arms outstretched calling me to hurry toward them. In one movement I was bundled into a cap gown and mask, our 100yard dash to the delivery room must, I am sure, have set a new world record.

Yvonne looked very scared and pale laying there on the delivery bed, her whole body trembling as she grabbed for my hand in my excitement all sense of pain had gone, I put it down to the adrenaline rushing through my body. Yvonne's hold on me increased as the length and strength of each contraction arrived, all my fingers began turning white, as I struggled desperately to comfort her. After almost thirty minutes of verbal abuse and language unbecoming of her, and at eleven o'clock precisely, the cries of a new-born baby echoed through the corridors of the Maternity Department of Northgate hospital.

Yvonne has at last given birth to our second baby Another baby girl, and boy is she a peach. She has deep brown eyes, fair hair and like her sister weighed in at an amazing 7 pounds 10 ounces, no wonder the pain was so bad. The fear and uncertainty we both had of never being able to have more children, has at long last been lifted from our hearts. "It is Wednesday September 19th. 1979 we are proud to announce the safe arrival of our second child a Girl"!

There were, I am pleased to say, no complications and both mother and child are doing well. After about 22 minutes or so it was suggested that I go home for a few hours, the excitement was too overwhelming I could hardly wait to spread the news. I was told that I could return in the evening, but for now it was imperative mother and baby were able to get some rest. I asked if I would be able to bring my elder daughter in to see her mum and sister, the answer given was a prompt "Yes!" As I left the hospital I felt on top of the world, nothing could spoil this glorious day.

Visiting hours could not have come quick enough, Anne-Marie was excited at the fact she was about to see her mum and new sister as much as I was. Although Yvonne and I were a little worried that she might be jealous or resentful toward the baby, well she was now no longer the centre of attraction, but those worries were unfounded. Yvonne was asleep when we walked onto the ward and was unsure of where she was when Anne-Marie excitedly woke her.

I was unable to prevent her from jumping into the arms of her tearful mother, so she could give her a kiss and cuddle. Anne-Marie's mind then turned to wanting to see her sister in her excitement almost upturned the fishbowl as the mothers call it (transparent plastic trolley cot). As we were unable to make our minds up on what name to call the baby, we asked Anne-Marie if she would like to choose a name.

Wow" she proudly cried jumping excitedly up and down. Then after a few moments; said "let's call her Amanda Louise Cherry" done. Through all the excitement we had lost all sense of time, once again time had caught up with us, hospitals visiting has ended and as expected there are a few tears there was not enough time to hold Amanda as we are forced to say our goodbye's. All the way home Anne-Marie could not stop talking about having a baby sister, she was one proud little girl and I was not going to take that feeling away from her. Yvonne's parents have been looking after Anne-Marie while this has been going on, I have no idea how I would have managed without their help although I have not said it publicly, I love them for it. I slept well all night and woke just after 9 am as I slowly crawled out of bed a large bundle of letters fell with a thump on the door mat. Most were bills of one kind or another, so I left them unopened as you do, at this moment, the first thing on my mind was a cup of coffee followed by a cigarette.

The coffee was great but....in the excitement of yesterday I had smoked nearly all my cigarettes, so, after a few well-chosen words I trundled off to the garage and bought another two hundred cigarettes including the traditional cigar although I had no one to hand it to. As no one else smokes in the family I just bought one for me. After a refreshing mug of coffee and a cigarette, I telephone the hospital to see how mother and child had been over night.

The nurse told me that both had slept well, and that Yvonne had just finished feeding Amanda, Yvonne was going to feed Amanda herself rather than bottle feeding. The hospital had given Yvonne a beast pump to extract milk for night feeds apparently so, Yvonne told me it was quite a painful task. I then told her I would be in to see Yvonne this afternoon and if possible, please could she pass on the message. I arrived a little before visiting time so that I could buy Yvonne a box of Maltesers which are her favourite sweets. The corridor was packed with husbands and relatives, all anxious for the doors to open and allow us through, when finally, the doors did open; the rush was so incredible it was almostfrightening. It reminded me of the chaotic stampede you see at Harrods in London when the Department store has a January Sale. People veraciously pushing and shoving their way through as if there were not tomorrow, oblivious of their surroundings it was a miracle that no one was seriously injured.

Yvonne was lying on top of the bed and holding Amanda in her arms as I walked onto the ward, "Hi! Darling how are you feeling?" Amanda stirred as I gave them both a kiss, Yvonne sank well into the pillow that was supporting her back. "A little sore and rather week, otherwise not too bad" she replied. I felt something was really worrying her, she appeared pre-occupied with other matters.

Eventually she told me that the doctors were a little concerned about the amount of blood loss during the birth, I admit she did look rather drawn and pale. With plenty of bed rest and lots of fluids that loss would soon be made up I'm sure, but I still had this niggly feeling there was something else worrying her, it then became clear apparently the doctors were also concerned Yvonne's immune system for measles was rather low, so they decided to vaccinate her, hearing that I too became concerned but for varied reasons what affect would this have on the baby as Yvonne was intending to breast feed.

The doctor assured us it was safe breast feeding would be fine, the baby would not suffer any ill effects or harm the baby. Yvonne placed the baby gently in her cot, after a long hard stretch and a big yawn she settled down without opening her eyes. The best news was that Yvonne has been told that tomorrow if there were no complications, they would both be allowed to return home. It will be strange hearing the cries of a small baby again around the bungalow, to become once more accustomed to the smell of boiling nappies.

There will be the continual visits from friends and neighbours, having seen the world's best form of advertisement for the arrival of a new baby. Washing line full of brand-new nappies these and many other things we shall have to contend with, "Great isn't it"! There goes that blasted bell again; time to go home, still Yvonne looked quite tired so I kissed her goodbye and told her I would call again tonight.

As I walked out of the ward, I realised that in all the time I was there I had not once held or cuddled the baby since she was born. That will change when I return tonight, my main problem now was to get home before Anne-Marie finishes school as I promised to pick her up and take her to see her new Sister. I can hardly wait to see the look on her pretty little face, as I tell her that mum and her new sister might be coming home tomorrow. Anne-Marie's excitement on hearing the news was fantastic she almost strangled me to death, she wasted no time in letting her nanny and granddad know. It was decided that when Yvonne and the baby are discharged from the hospital, they will stay with her mother for the first 10 days. The most important thing a man learns in marriage if nothing else, is that you never argue with your mother-in-law, it can get you into deep trouble and any way you can never win.

Today September 21st. 1979, is a big day for us all, it is the beginning of the biggest adventure of her new life. The doctor has now informed us, we are now clear to go home, but there is of course, just a couple of jobs to do before setting off we must give the baby a name and that is a job for Anne-Marie as it is her sister after all.

Anne-Marie did not take exceptionally long to produce a name, we will call her "Amanda Louise" what a beautiful name to call her, now we can register the birth of "Amanda Louise Cherry" we can then go home. There is one regret however I hold when looking back, it was not having a camera to photograph this wonderful miracle but neither did I the same regret also when Anne-Marie was born. So sadly, we missed having a photographic record of either as babies, if only we had the power to turn back the clocks "Ah well that's life."

Chapter Four

HOME AT LAST

I t was nearly 5 pm in the afternoon when we finally arrived at mother's front door, Anne-Marie dived out of the car ran inside the house jumping up and down saying "Nanny; Nanny; Nanny" I picked the baby's name! we are calling her "Amanda Louise" then dashed out the door nearly knocking us all over.

Amanda was sound asleep, and Yvonne was tired and exhausted as she had been up since 6 am. Before I had taken the cases from the boot of the car, Yvonne was whisked into the front room which had now been turned into a bedroom. It was pointed out that because of the lack of space, I will have to stay at home, every night but would have my meals there.

As you can imagine I was not too happy about that but what, it will only be for 10 days I can hack that. Although tea was made, and we were all hungry, Yvonne was more interested in having a proper cup of tea. After we had eaten, I decided to have an early night, there were a couple of things I had to do before going to bed anyway, and now was as good a time as any. Yvonne has had a bath, Amanda has been fed and is asleep in the front room, and Anne-Marie is finally asleep in bed upstairs so there is nothing else for me to do but go home.

The events of the past few days had taken its toll and I woke to find that I had overslept, as I dived out of bed, I found myself being propelled headlong across the bedroom. My feet became entangled in the bedclothes and ended up crumpled in a heap alongside the wardrobe painful as it was, I managed to sort myself out and after a cup of coffee and a fag, I was ready to face the world and the ear bashing I was in for as a result for sleeping in. The sun was shining brightly, a refreshing cool breeze prevented it from getting too warm in fact, this was a perfect day.

The doctor was in the middle of examining Yvonne and the baby when I arrived, he was pleased to see that Yvonne was being forced to rest and gave mother-in-law his full blessing (what a creep)! He was not happy with Amanda's condition though, the yellowish pigmentation of her skin and in her eyes, told him that she was very jaundiced. He was incredibly surprised that the hospital allowed Amanda home in that condition, as normally she would have stayed in till at least it had cleared. Still, he quickly put our minds at ease by telling us to keep her in the sunshine in a few days, she should be right as rain.

Amanda had also not slept well last night; the reason it was thought may have been due to the change in the environment and hopefully will quickly settle down. After the doctor had finished his examinations, he had a few words with mum and left. I asked if I could hold Amanda and give her a cuddle, this was denied, and I was told I could hold her later. This problem was to occur several times again, in different forms, either Amanda was asleep, or she has just been fed and changed. No matter what; I was being prevented from bonding Amanda and that hurt, I could not understand why. This constant refusal to allow me the right to hold my own child was becoming increasingly hurtful, even telling Yvonne about it had no effect. All I got from her was mum is only thinking of Amanda, I just wish her mum would butt-out and allow us to get on with both of our lives as a family.

We have been home for almost a week, and still I have not been allowed to hold Amanda. I feel so angry I want to explode and hit out at someone but what would that achieve, so instead I decided to storm out of the house. If I am not good enough to hold my own child, then I am not good enough to enter Yvonne's mothers house. "Stupid I know but that is how my mind was working."

I think one would really call my actions as unacceptable jealousy so thinking about it will need to apologise for my outburst. I had not been home long when the telephone rang, it was Yvonne. She wanted to know what the problem was, "You don't listen do you Yvonne." I said, I told you earlier in the week that I was angry because, since coming out of hospital your mother has, I feel done everything in her power to prevent me from holding or even cuddling Amanda." The ability to start a meaningful relationship to bond as a father should with a new Child, which was being systematically removed from me I had become so, upset I found it hard holding back, the tears. Yvonne began crying as she begged me to return. "Surely, we can work this problem out?" she spoke. but I was far too angry at this stage to discuss the issue any further and hung up after a few hours on my own I eventually calmed down enough to call Yvonne and apologised, I told her that I would see her tomorrow morning until then give Anne-Marie and Amanda a hug and kiss for me and sleep tight.

The following morning was clearly not easy for me and quite rightly so, the outburst and the comments I had made was completely out of order and required a serious and heartfelt apology to the whole family. As each day passed Amanda's colour improved this was to the delight of everyone; but I am sure if there had been clearly no sign of improvement, the doctor was seriously thinking about the possibility of having Amanda admitted to hospital.

The days passed quite quickly and finally we were once more home, a family under our very own roof. The torment endured these past few weeks had finally ended. Family life can now become normal, whatever normal is. Anne- marie was playing in the back garden, Yvonne was busy washing clothes in the old hot point rotating washing machine, a relic from years gone by and yes it had the old hand cranked wooden rollers that squeezed so much water out it made clothes stiff as a board.

We had several close misses with our fingers, but we really could not fault it, best thing since sliced bread at the time. When washing was hung out to dry it only took half an hour or so to dry. Amanda was sound asleep in her cot; I was outside painting the front step in the porch way with dark green none slip floor paint.

Yvonne's mum phoned to see how we all were and how. Naturally, Amanda was startled, boy has she got a pair of lungs on her or what? I recall we had been home for about two weeks when we were aware Amanda's feeding habits started to change just taking a bottle clearly proved to be insufficient for her needs it appeared that three hourly feeds of four ounces of milk was not satisfying enough and were recommended to maybe try adding half a baby rusk biscuit to her last bottle of the day.

"Wow"! that made a dramatic change something of value a tip to place in an ever-increasing suggestion boxes, after three weeks had passed, we noticed that Amanda had become very agitated and off her feeds she kept on crying and nothing, but nothing we did seemed to pacify her. The harder we tried the task of trying to pacify her the worse she became, a strange red rash starting to appear on her tummy and as we watched; it appeared to be spreading rapidly covering her whole body, face, neck, under arms, legs and down her arms. Panic set in both Yvonne and I had never seen this type of rash before nor the speed with which it took hold, Amanda was still crying whatever this rash was it must have been quite painful; we both have never heard any child cry in the past like this. In shear and out of total fear and desperation rang her GP's surgery the horrendous screaming could be heard by the receptionists and we were instructed to come at once to see her doctor.

By the time we got to the Surgery Amanda was covered from head to foot, the rash looked very much like measles or possibly Chicken pox and was obviously very sore looking as well as painful even to touch hence the way she was screaming. The effect this had on those who were waiting in the surgery was quite concerning and certainly made aware by the horrified whispering emanating from all those in the waiting room, which by the way was only 12 feet by 9 feet including the chairs.

Thankfully, we did not have too long to wait and were called within a few minutes, as we entered the doctors consulting room, we were met by Dr Kelly young-looking man he had a quiet posh voice which sounded if he was from a well to do Family or had during his educational upbringing attended Oxford or Cambridge. I recall that he was smartly dressed in a darkish suit, and round his neck lay his stethoscope; his desk was clear of any clutter only a note pad ink Pen and blotting paper. He had a black telephone at almost arm's length away to the right of his desk, wash basin and medical cupboards to the left of the room and a large slightly opened window directly behind him. A stainless steel examination trolley covered with two white sheets one large draped the trolly and a small sheet partially covered a kidney tray and a few other items existed just behind the door where the patients enter and two chairs to the left or front of table.

Dr Kelly asked us to take a seat he could see that Amanda was in considerable distress and that Yvonne and I were in shock, while we were explaining the rudiments of Amanda's symptoms over the last 12 – 24 hours the rash began to disappear her screaming subsided and she lay in our arms calm relaxed and peaceful. Suddenly without warning Amanda went rigid her head thrust back her little arms went into spasm the right arm outstretched her left arm pulled toward her chest: she was clenching her tiny hands shut her whole-body began twisting as she began to almost roll up into a ball, she did not stop there as we watched Amanda's eyes roll back showing the whites of her eyeballs; it looked horrific. Her whole body then started shaking and she again began crying as if in pain.

Yvonne and I were frightened and emotionally scared out of our minds, all kinds of bad negative thoughts including is she dying? Dr. Kelly asked "how did you get to the surgery"? "We drove" I said. "Good!" he replied, I could see that Amanda disposition was creating him serious concerns. Apart from an occasional head scratching, the biting of his lips and odd flipping through a medical book was giving him no answers. Dr. Kelly confirmed he had no idea why Amanda was presenting symptoms of a large full rash that covered he entire torso, and as one watch disappeared as quickly as it came.

Amanda's convulsing was also concerning the power exerting was tremendous it was impossible to depict the finishing point before the next one began, her whole body wreathing and uncontrollable jerking made it almost impossible to keep hold of her. The high-pitched screaming was deafening when breathing stopped she was turning every shade of red and blue you can think of even thumping her on the back to get her to breathe again was a real struggle. "I need you to take Amanda to Gt. Yarmouth hospital now!" Dr Kelly Said, "I will just write out a report and will give it to you to take with you." he said. "While I am doing this, can you please wait in the waiting room outside."

Chapter Five

DASH TO GT. YARMOUTH GENERAL HOSPITAL

T he traffic I am pleased to say was seriously light for the time of day, we were driving through every traffic light. "Clearly" God was on our side as each light turned green, we were able to get to the hospital within 25 minutes, it was trying to find a parking spot and as I was not familiar with the area I started to panic. I found a spot in George Street behind St. Georges Theatre and at the rear of the hospital, as we made our way to the Children's Ward.

We walked through 2 large green wooden gates, in front and up against the left-hand wall were four large wire crates full of bedding sheets mixed in with large red, yellow sacks etc. Next to them and not caged off were 5 large and unsecured oxygen cylinders the tops were painted white, 2 were obviously in use as they were connected to taps on the wall. It appeared that health and safety issues were being flouted, none of the oxygen cylinders were restrained with strapping and if accidently knocked would most certainly have fallen over.

Baring slightly to the left was a ramp or slipway going up one floor and further round to the right a staircase going down. It was then that it dawned on me we had come through the tradesmen service area, well that is about right I always thought I was a second-class person. There were 2 green doors on our right one was what look like a training room, the other was attached to what resembled a castle's turret. As we opened the turret door, we were hit in the face with a strong smell of disinfectant, so strong was it that it felt like we were being disinfected before reaching our destination. We proceeded to climb the stairs as they wound their way up to the right, the stone steps were smooth shiny and seriously worn smooth in the middle from years of use by people walking up and down certainly, a health hazard in my opinion.

The only light at the bottom of the staircase; emanated from two panes of glass in the green door and from small eighteen by eleven-inch window, as you rounded the corner, on reaching the top of the steps we were met by a wooden gate bolted and above that a small light bulb that did not have a shade. We opened the gate and walked through turning sharp left and a short corridor, as we headed toward the main children's ward two very young-looking nurses and the ward sister hurried to us and introduced themselves. "I am Sister Jordan, and this is Sandra our staff nurse with nurse Clair a first-year student, you must be "Mr and Mrs Cherry, hello!" and this little one must be Amanda. "Before we progress any further the nurses will book Amanda in," "While they do that would you both like something to drink?" "Yes please; week tea for me and a strong coffee for Malcolm thank you!" Sister Jordan was an extremely attractive young woman shoulder length brown hair she was slim accentuated by a very snug fitting dark blue short sleeved uniform with white edgings on both the sleeves and lapels a bright red belt pulled her waist in she was also waring flat shoes and black tights.

Amanda was fitting quite strongly and crying I found it hard struggling to hold her in my arms as she was twisting arching her back, we were taken to a large empty ward at the top of the stairs, we just walked up. The ward felt cold and damp, yet the radiators were on; but just warm as if they had just been turned on, apart from Amanda there were no other children every time you spoke your voice echoed even with 8 large cots.

Four exceptionally large windows each I would estimate over 9 feet tall and 4 foot-wide adorned the ward I would not be surprised if it were not them making the ward so cold, Sister Jordan informed us that Dr. Back is the wards senior Paediatric Consultant regrettably was out just now but was due back about 3 pm.

Amanda continues to be seriously suffering it has been over an hour since we arrived nothing has been done to stop her seizers, we asked if something could be Done to give her a rest as she seemed to be in a great deal of pain, we must wait for her to be seen by Dr. Back first he is aware of Amanda's needs. Dr Back arrived on the ward about 90 minutes or so after Amanda was admitted, maybe now Amanda could be given some medication. Yvonne and I were at breaking point Amanda was convulsing stronger with the start of every seizure, nothing was being done to try and stop or control them in some way we were drowning in our own emotions. We were both praying for a miracle, how long can Amanda go on before her heart decide no more the thought is just frightening. Dr Back finally arrived to examine Amanda and seeing what she was going through hit him quite hard, he at once drew up an urgent prescription to give Amanda. He seemed quite upset and could not be so apologetic, he has read the letter we gave from Doctor Kelly and remarked that he felt he had made some observations that puzzled even him. Checking her notes and letter, we brought from Dr. Kelly." The length Amanda was made to wait was in our minds just madness no one should be made to suffer if it were an animal suffering like this the humane thing to do would be to put it down.

Thankfully, Amanda is not an Animal she is a human being and as I said to Dr. Back she has rights, sadly so it seems have only now been acted on. Both Yvonne and I are close to breaking point we felt like there was no justice in the world, the nursing staff could see how upset we both were.

We were given no comfort in the hospitals ability to care for Amanda, we were oblivious to what was going on, no one spoke to us until now. Every 20 minutes or so a nurse would enter the ward look at Amanda, took her temperature Blood pressure pulse and finally recorded their observations on a monitoring form at the end of her cot and left.

Finally, Sister Jordan came and told us that it would be a little while longer for the medication to be sent from the Pharmacy department and so she suggested we have something to eat, Amanda was although it might not seem it, in good hands and you need to take a break! Reluctantly we agreed and went into Yarmouth it was also necessary Yvonne and I got some fresh air and chill out time, we found a small café just up from the hospital, where we were able to order food well sandwiches and a hot sugary drink.

Our thoughts were on what is happening to Amanda while we were not there, Yvonne and I were gone close to an hour and a half, well although we did not know it, we had chance to wind down and build up our energy for the next round. As we opened the tower door and began our ascent of the stairs, we could not hear Amanda's loud cries in fact the only noise of shouting and screaming was emanating from the main children's ward: it was surprising that we did not collide with any of the boisterous children running around. Entering the ward, we were Shocked to find Amanda had been placed on an IV drip, but strangely not in a place one would expect it to be.

What shook us was the drip had been placed on the top of her head and fixed with plaster of Paris, the IV site is better known as the Fontanel or the soft spot hence why it was fixed in plaster of Paris. The Staff nurse informed us that it was better there than in the back of her hand, Sister Jordan had to call a doctor who decided to place the IV on the top of her head because if it were in any other part of her body, it might become dislodged while she was convulsing.

Amanda appeared to be asleep, she was prescribed a strong dose of Valium and the seizures seemed to be under some control although not sadly completely as every now and then her body was reacting to something. Yvonne and I felt a great deal better as the change in Amanda was dramatic compared to how she was an hour or so ago, when we reluctantly left, we were very frightened on what we would come back to.

As a nurse entered the room the doorknob rattled loudly, it was loose and it made us both jump it also required some much-needed oiling or if not a Screwdriver to tighten the handle mechanism also it had a ghostly squeak. We were asked if we would like a cup of tea or coffee "Yes please, week tea for Yvonne and a strong coffee for me little milk with two Sugars thank you." As the nurse was leaving Sister Jordan came in, "hello Mr and Mrs Cherry!" Did you manage to find somewhere to eat close by? "Yes, thank you but we were not happy to find a Parking Ticket on the car when we returned."

Considering the trouble, we both were experiencing. Give the ticket to me and we will write to the commissioner and see if it can be waived on this occasion once we explain the background. Sister Jordan again apologised "I am sorry we took so long giving Amanda medication, but she had to be seen by a Dr, first." We were both simply happy that something had eventually been done, because Amanda's convulsions were so powerful and the length of time, she had to wait she had to be given an extremely high dose of Valium rectally we understand that it works amazingly fast.

When delivered Rectally. Dr. Back requested we see him unfortunately he was called away urgently so we might get to see him tomorrow sometime. Yvonne was to some degree still angry and said she did not want to speak to him at this moment in time. Hopefully, she will have calmed down by tomorrow.

On our arrival at the hospital this morning, we were stopped from going into see Amanda, it was clear to everyone things were not right. Amanda was literally screaming a type of scream not heard before, we were ushered into the nurse's office basically. The nurse's office was really split into two, one side used as an office the other side was a kitchen. As you entered there was to the left an exceptionally large window, in front of that a table covered in paper forms and folders. The window enabled nurses to keep a physical eye on the ward, a couple of uncomfortable looking wooden chairs placed around the table not that the nurses had much time to sit on them. To the left was a wash basin, fridge a small toaster and kettle making tea and coffee.

Sister Jordan was sitting at the table writing what looked like reports, as we entered; she closed the folder placing her pen on top as she slid round on the chair, she welcomed us, and we sat down "Tea, Coffee" "thank you but no" we were more concerned about Amanda, "why was she screaming?" I asked "Amanda has not had a good night!" Sister Jordan quickly replied, her seizures had dramatically increased in both strength and number, the reason for screaming was Dr's were concerned it might be Meningitis she was therefore undergoing her second lumber puncture and because of her status had to be forcibly restrained.

The procedure requires a patient to remain as still as possible, in Amanda's case this was proving quite difficult because of her seizures. Naturally, we were quite tearful, for her: apparently it is quite a traumatic procedure and not a very pleasant procedure for an adult, even less so for a baby to undergo this type of procedure at her early age, the pain alone can be frighteningly horrific. Clearly Amanda is unable to understand what was happening and the only way is to scream out.

Painfully there is nothing we can do; we are literally in the hands of the Dr's we Knew, clearly for now they were trying to discover the cause of Amanda's illness but to justify putting her through these painful procedures was we believe the right thing even though we were in my opinion being cruel. Yvonne and I have spent many soul-searching hours tearfully crying asking probing questions. questions without a single justifiable answer, watching Amanda suffering although they tried to assure us unsuccessfully, we might add that through all the moans and groans crying and screaming she is not feeling any pain "what a load of bollocks and bull shit!" seizures or no seizures the actions shown by Amanda on a minute by minute; second by second; and day by day proves to us she is in horrific sustained pain.

Yvonne and I were not allowed to attempt to cuddle Amanda after the lumber puncture procedure had been completed; a patient must lay still we understand for some twelve hours after undergoing a lumber puncture procedure. Amanda was therefore administered Valium this time by IV (intravenously) or to explain it better through the site in her head, today had begun badly; and we did not know if it was not going to get any better. After lunch we went directly to see Amanda, she was still well sedated and lying on her right side, we both lowered the side of the cot and sat down.

Yvonne took Amanda's hand it felt very cold her breathing seemed a little laboured, the concerns and anguish we had experienced just over ninety minutes or so ago still had some hold over us. Fear is the devil's playground it tends to eat and devour every fibre of our bodies; even though there were significant changes in Amanda's problem, our only defence is to lash out not only at each other but also, with hospital staff and those people most precious to us. Not a single day goes by where we ask ourselves:

- What did we do wrong?
- We are too slow in spotting serious underlying problems since her birth.
- Are we being punished for some wrongdoing?
- Could we have done better?
- Are we terrible parents)

Yvonne and I are really struggling we have nowhere to go, and we are both fighting for Amanda a desperately sick little girl who is start in life has been dealt a wicked hand. I would not class myself as a devout Christian but nonetheless I do consider myself a Christian, so where is this God, this so-called loving God who allows innocent Children to suffer? My belief in God in the whole ethos of faith in Christianity is being torn apart piece by piece, the strength I thought I had; is now strongly being put to the test. I desperately need to calm myself down, so, I said "Yvonne" I am going to have a fag in the courtyard downstairs, I might even have a stroll round the block; my whole body felt like jelly shacking as frustration and anger mixed.

On my return Sister Jordan was speaking to Yvonne telling her what had been going on, and that Amanda had a seriously bad night. The Dr's had been with her since four thirty this morning they gave her another Lumber puncture and sent the test to the Lab, when the results came back slightly abnormal, they felt they had to repeat the procedure that had just been started as we walked on to the ward hence the strange screaming, we heard when we came in.

Having that information did nothing to how we were feeling and why would it? It just made the pain we had hurt even more, anyway sister Jordan had come to take us to see doctor. Back this was supposed to have happened yesterday, but he was called away. Yvonne did not want to leave Amanda and was holding her hand tightly, so I went on my own, his consulting room was at the far end of the main ward.

I had not really taken much notice of the layout of the wards but nevertheless, what I did see reminded me of an old Victorian building inside, like those seen in "Carry on films" a kitchen at one end and doctor's consultation office the other, both can see what was going on in the ward. Sister Jordan knocked on the door and was beckoned to enter, the room looked quite spacey couple of chairs place just in front of a large consulting table with several types of coloured folders, a couple of thick medical books, one was open and resting on the one below. Loose papers randomly lay everywhere in fact one might say the desk was remarkably busy desk.

Behind the desk sat a middle-aged doctor, with grey thinning hair and wearing an unbuttoned jacketed Grey Suit white shirt and red tie. A black stethoscope hung round his neck, a pair of thick framed Glasses lay on an open book to his right, behind, a large untidy looking pin board full of posters and uninteresting medical forms you would likely have seen in a GP surgery or Dentist waiting room. Small windowpanes 8 in all no larger than 6 by 8, dust particles normally not seen with a naked eye could be clearly seen floating around highlighted by the extremely bright sun as it poured through the panes of glass.

The walls had sometime in the past been painted or rather whitewashed, and in places appeared to be flaking off. In various places looked somewhat stained a pale yellowish colour as if at some point cupboards or filing cabinets had been placed there for an exceptionally long time and eventually moved. "Take a seat please, I will be with you in a second."

As I sat down the door opened; a nurse entered carrying a tray of tea's and coffee," Ah thank you nurse, just what the doctor ordered, he chuckled to himself." "Good afternoon, Mr. Cherry! your wife not with you?" I informed him she wanted to stay with Amanda, and he seemed quite happy with that, "did you know Mr. Cherry when I first heard you're name it seemed familiar. As a young man, just finishing my internship, I recall seeing a Mr and Mrs Cherry while living in the west indies." he said "Your father I recall was a member of the British Armed Forces I believe?" "Did he not hold the commission of a warrant Officer, Regimental Sargent Major if I recall rightly?" "That's right" I said ("Well it is truly a small world we live in.") "strange" he said, how the brain works in mysterious ways.

"I remember now" he said, "I was about to leave the hospital for something to eat when you were hurriedly rushed in." "You were screaming very loudly I recall not surprisingly as two of your leg bones had broken the skin and were protruding about 3 inches". "I was the paediatrician you saw; I was studying Tropical Diseases at the time," anyway enough of the reminiscing he said. "I have examined Amanda" he said. "To be truthful Mr. Cherry; I am seriously struggling to find a possible cause." "Therefore, I need to keep her here, as clearly the seizure urgently need to be brought under full control."

Finding the reason for her seizures must take priority, "So, I have written up a Medication of drugs which can be given by IV as and when required." Dr. Back also told me that he has recommended she be given Epilim to try on Amanda, its an anti-convulsant medication successfully used to control Epilepsy. As you have no doubt seen Amanda has an IV drip to the top of her head, the reason for this placement is due to the fact Amanda's seizures are so violent there is an extremely high possibility she will remove the IV if placed in normal sites. With that in mind I decided it may be prudent to place it there instead, she has now been given a 10-milligram ampule of Valium Rectally it seems to have partially calmed the seizures down and the reason she is sleeping now. Amanda's seizures are still quite prominent as there is still visible jerking of limbs and head. The worst was yet to come, I must be incredibly careful and choose my words within Quotes as they were spoken to me.

"I would strongly recommend that in view of the fundamental problems Amanda is experiencing, both you and Mrs Cherry should consider leaving Amanda here!" "Go home;" and forget you ever had her" after what seemed quite a lengthy pause, I said in a bewildered response… "EXCUSE ME." … "Doctor Back I am not too sure, I caught what you just said and asked he repeat it.?" "Did you just say Leave Amanda here; go home and forget we ever had her?!!!" He said "YES!" that is my recommendation.

"Hearing that statement felt like someone had just plunged a red-hot knife into my chest" the pain I felt at this point is indescribable, any; yes, any respect for doctor Back I may have; had just flew out the small windows. If it had been at all physically possible, he would have closely followed closely behind, I was fuming my whole body began to shake uncontrollably, my head felt as if it were about to explode; I really felt physically sick. This was a qualified professor of medicine publicly and unprofessionally recommending abandoning a child to medical science, I wish I had a tape recorder on me. I would have had no hesitation in reporting him for unprofessional conduct, ending his career in an instant or physically assaulting him in public.

I was ragingly angry; I had clearly lost it and my fatherly emotions took over, quickly standing bolt upright the backs of my Legs caught the chair behind me propelling it against a cabinet. I leant menacingly over his table my face inches from his, he was so startled he reared back away from his table pushing himself back into his winged leather chair. "That child," doctor I said is my daughter; she is my flesh my Blood" "How dare you think you can play "God" I ask you do you really think you're a doctor?" "I would never ever agree to leaving her here forgetting she ever existed, and you call yourself a Dr?" "Well do yah!?" "You're nothing but a pathetic little shit." I place you now on notice, you have made a real enemy of me, you have lost any trust I had in you and will be constantly looking over your shoulder watching every decision you make from now on" I told him. As I left his office, I slammed the door so hard I'm surprised the glass did not smash.

"I was physically shaking with rage, the veins in my neck felt like they were going to burst. I had to leave before I did something I would later regret later, even Sister Jordan could not believe what Back had strongly recommended we should think of doing. Sister Jordan followed closely behind calling for me to stop. Tears were rolling down my cheeks it takes a lot to make me cry, this sadly is one of them. Do you know what; hindsight is a marvellous thing the action I took today at the hospital was so very wrong and completely out of character I wish it had never happened, I allowed the anger and Frustration inside me take control my body. I totally blanked out the fact there were young children on the ward, and I must have frightened them. The anger I have; was in the words of Sister Jordan justified; she would most likely have reacted the same way had she been in the same shoes, but I should have considered where I was and the fact there were small children about.

Yvonne like me was angry and upset when I told her, the damage was done and I would have to face any dressing down regarding my outburst. Sister Jordan entered the ward carrying a chair and sat down beside us, she was very calming and sympathetic she could feel how upset we were; in her defence she had a job to do. She was unable to speak out but assured us that if they were in charge things may have been handled differently, a tray of biscuits tea and coffee arrived. We spoke for over an hour, by the end of the talking we somehow ended up on first name basis. Strange how a little thing like a cup of tea can calm someone down, it must have been the sugar, we told her, how over the last 12 - 24 hours we felt alone we had no one to turn too and how frightened we both were. Then to be told by Dr. Back to forget we ever had Amanda was the last straw.

Amanda's strong sedation would keep her asleep for the rest of the day, Sister Jordan suggested we might consider going home "return tomorrow" she said "They would phone us if there was any change in her wellbeing. It was after all 8.30 pm. We had Anne -Marie at home or rather staying with her nanny. No matter what is going on in our lives we have two children and what we don't want to see happen, is that one suffers or miss out on family life.

Driving home, we decided to get something to eat, there was a chippie in Gorleston, we have passed by many times and as luck would have it. They were still open, ordering chicken and chips, we sat in the car and ate them boy they smelt so good and inviting and tasted fantastic. The chip shop must have been on the point of closing as we arrived, and we were given a more than generous helping of chips as for the chicken the aroma was out of this world. The sizes of each chicken half were massive and had been cooked on a rotisserie. The skins were crispy golden brown the meat so succulent as you cut into it the meat came off in strings, the windscreens of the car front and back became misted up even with them lowered.

Yvonne and I would stop there every night and order chicken and chips they were that good including a pot of hot mushy peas, on occasions I would buy a pot of spicy Curry sauce. It was quite late when we eventually got home. So, we both decided it would be much better to pay her a visit tomorrow, the confrontation with Dr. Back had drained us both. We never even made a bedtime drink but went and crashed out, even though we were worn out last night it felt like we had not slept a single wink, as we awoke at 6,30 am in the morning. Yvonne telephoned her mother just before 8 am this morning to tell her we were on our way, we would update her on what happened yesterday. The altercation Malcolm had with Dr. Back, we felt was clearly the wrong time to speak about then and there.

Anne-Marie was also up, it was brilliant to see her as she came bounding down the path toward us. With all that was going on we fell into the very thing I was trying to avoid, and that was forgetting momentarily to include Anne-marie in the discussion about her sister. Anne-marie was so excited "I'm all grown up now!"

Being grown up meant she witnessed the raw tearful emotions emanating from us both, what she could not understand; were the tears and crying as we spoke. "Clearly not so grown up as she thought"

We eventually arrived at the hospital at 11.49 am in the morning only to be met with crying and screaming from Amanda's room, Sister Jorden called us over "Just before we walked into the room, she had not had a comfortable night. There was a strange look in her eyes a look of apprehension and I supposed worry what I might do after yesterday's escapades with doctor. Back. We were taken into the office and offered a drink of tea and coffee, in fact they do this to every visiting parent. It makes you wonder if they place some sort of calming medication into the drink before delivering nasty news reports, Sister Jordan explained "Amanda did not have a good night and had yet again, suffered With Gran-Mal seizures and to sedate her she was prescribed 10 milligrams a rectal Valium ampule: doctors had been working on Amanda since the early hours and were in the middle of giving her a second Lumber Puncture.

The results of the first one showed a possible abnormality, but were not too sure, so they are taking a second one and that is what they were doing when we arrived. It was rather annoying that we were not contacted to inform us that Amanda had been bad through the night, then to be told that she was having a second procedure to investigate if there was a problem with the first procedure got the old heckles up. I found it exceedingly difficult controlling my emotion but this time I was not going to scare other patients, we did not have to wait long, the Dr's finish the second Lumber Puncture and left the ward. I'm not sure how long it will take to have the result come back, sister Jordon reckoned they will have them back this afternoon. Amanda was given another ampule of Valium again as her seizures were quite strong, doctors were finding it difficult to see when one seizure ended and the next one began this issue continued even under heavy sedation.

"I have been trying to compile a daily diary while we sat with her," the fact we found it was not easy to distinguish one seizure from another for me it was so, So, frightening. To begin with, I'll be honest I had to guestimate most of the Time initially, but then who said it was going to be easy. after watching her closely after about an hour of scrutiny, I decided to make her arm dropping as a single fit. In the first hour using the dropping arm movement as a guide to Amanda's seizures, I counted at least 534, grand mal seizures. x's that by 7 the Time the number of hours we were with her totals 3,738 that's just today.

"How her little body could cope was a miracle," my heart was breaking I cried tear's as I counted each one and her little face turned red each time as she tensed her legs pulling them up almost onto her chest stiffening of arms with one bending toward her face twisting her head to the right while jerking and crying as if she was in pain, she seemed to strain as if constipated trying to go to the toilet which in turn seemed to stop her breathing hence the red face.

The shock of seeing this was too much to handle something had to be seriously done her little heart cannot take anymore, Dr's prescribe a barbiturate drug "Phenobarbitone" I don't think it had a nice taste as Amanda pulled a horrible face. Amanda was not showing any changes in her seizures slowing down, in fact, if anything they appeared to have increased in strength as well. The duty doctor was called, he saw how bad she was she and drew up another prescription of "Phenobarbitone." We thought it would not be wrong of us in asking if they were any nearer to finding out what was coursing Amanda's

Seizures, he told us that they were still awaiting results of tests taken and once they had been looked at by Dr. Back he would inform us of the next step forward. I would not be surprised if his attituded after the altercation in his office would now affect the speed of his action. Naturally, we were not happy and the longer the not knowing will; in our opinion increase damage to Amanda. If in truth they have no idea, then their next step surely would be to try and find someone else who may be able to find answers. A question I have put to all the Dr's including Dr. Back. Yvonne and I were increasingly becoming more agitated and angrier by the minute, in fact we felt we were really fighting for Amanda's life and we we're losing. I'm beginning to think the altercation with Dr Back about leaving Amanda forgetting about her angered him and therefore, he is punishing us by holding back on the results. (Deep down I knew this was for me frustratingly grabbing at straws), after all it has only been two days.

Before we left to go home Sister Jordan came in and said "Amanda was a little dehydrated and wanted to put a nasal gastric tube into her stomach, that was they could feed her without worrying how much she has had." The speed with which it was inserted blew my mind, then with a syringe she was able to check if it were in her tummy, with the tube in the correct place it was held in place by a thin strip of clear tape. We decided as they were in the process of dishing out tea in the main ward we would wait till Amanda had been fed, nurse Saunders had been assigned to look after Amanda. She was very thin deep brown eyes her hair was a deep brown tied tightly into a bun; she was carrying a jug of hot water a syringe and a 200mil bottle of milk, she placed the bottle in the jug to warm up the milk while she checked Amanda's arm band to make sure, she had the correct patient.

Nurse Saunders checked to confirm the tube was in Amanda's tummy by drawing up some bile from her tummy, with all the checks required being done Amanda was able to have a feed a large Syringe was connected to the top of the tube and the milk poured into that, surprising how quickly it went all finished in less than 5 minutes. After a feed nurse Saunders took Amanda's observation or as they call it (op's). Her temperature was slightly high suggesting she may have a bug or something, her pulse was very erratic but that was clearly in my opinion down to the seizures. If nothing else could go wrong today as we left the ward there was a tremendous crack It made everyone jump, you might have guessed thunder followed by almost a heavy Tropical type of rainstorm. It just had to happen to us as we left the Hospital a further example of punishment. Leaving Amanda was extremely hard for us both, we had lost all control and the ever-increasing mental fear we of being parted from her.

On the Journey home we had time to reflect on the day's events, the first question Every morning when we arrived "How has Amanda been over night"? Then response was always the same "she has had a restless night and was given rectal Valium," Dr Back is coming in to see her about dinner time which was his normal ward walk. We then ask has there been any results back which give any answers to why she was like this, naturally there were none currently but doctor Back might have some news. As we entered the ward Amanda was having a large seizer, she began crying out as usual as if in pain and jerking quite violently.

Unfortunately, Sister Jordan was off work suffering from I understand food poisoning and had to go home. That will explain why we have not seen her Anyway, we called the ward sister, but she was handing over to the day staff, there was something different looking about Amanda today, she was very puffy and that worried us both; was this another symptom of the problem, her body seamed somewhat bloated and the child lying in the cot… was nothing at all like Amanda. When the night staff had finished their hand over report came and had a word with us, we asked why Amanda was so bloated?

Apparently again she had been convulsing overnight and the night staff called the duty paediatric doctor a Mr. Patel, all we know about him is he is a young man, about 27 years of age from India and with a soft speaking voice some of the nurses' comments suggest they find him irresistibly handsome, all I am interested in is knowing what he is like as a doctor! Doctor. Patel was quite horrified I understand to see the status Amanda was in, and prescribed Valium, they seem to use this medication with all types of problems and in my opinion whatever that is worth a miracle worker. Even so he has also written up some steroid treatment to see if that might have some affect in controlling her seizures, and it is that which has made her so puffy.

Keeping a registered account of her seizures in a diary was not an easy thing to do, the problem occurs when we went home at the end of the day. Naturally, the counting ceases until we both return the following morning, but I feel it to be a necessary and worthwhile exercise. The shock comes when you count the number at days end, to give you an idea; today the number of seizures from 7 am in the morning to 8.35 tonight totalled over 1906. No two days are ever the same: on day 3 the end total reached a massive 11214, and that is only an estimated number due to difficulties already explained. What is so frightening is the fact that we are not with her 24/7 and unaware of the numbers of seizures Amanda has possibly had due to the fact we we're not there clearly will dramatically affect the final figure.

Amanda has now been in Gt. Yarmouth Hospital just over a week, quite a lot of tests had been carried out; tests on which we were consulted. You can imagine the anger we felt when told us they have been giving her steroids without even Consulting with us first, she looked a right mess the hospital name band was

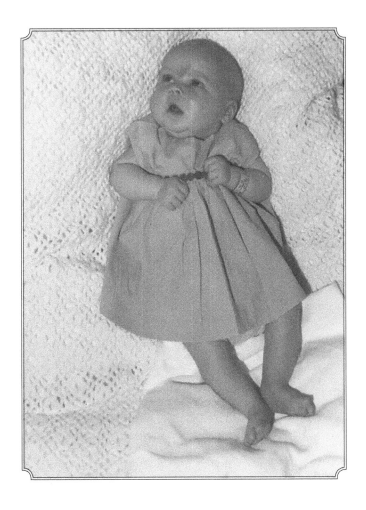

Chapter Six

THE SEARCH
FOR A CAUSE

Amanda has been a patient in Gt. Yarmouth general children's Ward for over three weeks, she has been prodded, poked, stabbed with needles on every part of her body still they have no idea what the problem is or what the cause might be. All the tests conducted we have now been informed were to end the possible contraction of "Meningitis," the first results from the Lumber Punctures showing a possible abnormality, had doctors and the hospital and medical clinicians slightly concerned so hence the reason to do another test.

Naturally at the time they kept their concerns to themselves, evidently because of our mental and emotional status at the time. Any confrontation especially from me would certainly have helped the search for the cause, and no help to Amanda. The relief on the faces of staff was quite clear when

Meningitis was ruled out, especially the nursing staff they knew they were on the front line for my anger and chastisement not including me in what they were looking for and why they were putting Amanda through her ordeals. Even now that we know is not a comfort as we are still in limbo land, my feelings remain the same the continued belief is you cannot find the problem then take her to a hospital that can!

Today Amanda was given a new Anti – Convulsant medication, "Epanutin" this we were told was possibly the start of several anti-convulsant drugs that can be given to help combat Epileptic Seizures. Naturally with Amanda's seizures it would be trial and error, but they had to start somewhere. If we were ever to pray more for this drug to work for Amanda, then it is certainly at this very moment, if there really is a passionate God out there and listening "Please, oh please hear our prayer? help Amanda and allow this drug to work. Help doctors and nurses alike conquer these fits "Amen!"

Today Amanda's seizures topped eighteen hundred and two, so giving Epilim fail to work for her. So far putting Amanda on Epanutin may prove problematic too. There appears to be no noticeable effect it may well take a few days to take hold, like all things in this life you must be patient and that goes for some drugs work also. I am known to be a patient person but since Amanda has been ill that patience is not as forthcoming as one would like; we have seen our child who remember; we struggled seven long years to give birth too, now is fighting for survival, as are we on her behalf?

"Please can someone explain to us the reasons why we should be patient?" I'll tell you now "I will die for my family no second thought, to see a small child a human being having to suffer as she has you can take patience and shove it where the sun can't shine," The sooner people in this hospital and elsewhere realise and understand that; the happier I'll be. Every time a paediatrician enters Amanda's ward the first question past my lips is, "have you had any results back from you're constant testing as to what is happening to Amanda?" and their answer is always the same "NO" "then why will you not send her to a hospital that might have the equipment to get those answers. Or frankly do you sadistically get a kick out of watching young children like Amanda suffering?"

"Sorry doctor. That's out of order and uncalled for, please forgive me for that outburst, I know that you are struggling to find reasons for Amanda's problem. I am so frustrated with the negativity of results; I have just totalled Amanda's fits as having reached a frighteningly 235,494 since being admitted to Gt. Yarmouth Hospital. Naturally, this figure excludes any seizures prior to her being admitted, working on the principles of estimation before going into hospital I guestimate that Amanda had a staggering total of at least 1,000 give or take a 100 or so. I am convinced the nursing staff have not had time through the night to sit and count them

Well, it is the 12th of October Friday morning 10.30 am, we were told that Amanda was going to have an x-ray taken at about 10.50 am. The doctors are looking to see if Amanda had unfortunately a possible tumour "God please I beg you don't let it be that!" "My younger sister Christine at the age of 8yrs died from a brain tumour, it proved to be a lingering and painful death as I recall." We were told that the results would take about 30 minutes, gratefully I'm pleased to say that was the results of the results came back negative.

Amanda was being sent to Norfolk and Norwich Hospital; we understand Gt. Yarmouth's children's ward is having a paint up. There I was thinking had given up and were sending her to another hospital in a sense getting a second opinion, or even a fresh set of eyes that might find something they had missed. But no, it was because there are no paediatric doctors at

Lowestoft hospital, what a load of twaddle they have a children's ward there it really makes no sense at all sending her to Norwich. Anyway, that will happen on Monday she will be taken by Ambulance at around 2 pm in the afternoon.

Unfortunately, they are only insured to take one parent with her, so that meant I had to follow in the car. It was no problem as I would have found it quite difficult getting home again. Amanda was still knocking out the seizures, so Yvonne told me when I eventually found the Children's ward. I found it quite difficult unbelievably having to follow coloured line painted on most of the hospital walls or along the floor each having a designated ward or department, red to one area yellow to another blue somewhere else.

"I hate to think just how someone who happens to be colour blind manages it. must be a complete and utterly confusing nightmare," then I am not colour. blind and it was confusing to me. I did eventually manage to find a short cut to the side of the hospital that faced on to the main road, the parking area was at night times was empty all but three cars. The barriers to the car park only allowed drivers to exit, so on my arrival I was forced to drive the car completely. round the perimeter of the hospital. The ward was massive the first thing I noticed in the layout was the conveniently placed nurse's station, and as I entered there was a wall to my left with an exceptionally large window and to the right in a half circle quite small isolation rooms with the major ward further round. There was not a single blind spot, it was light and airy although I would. point out it that tell-tell clinical smell but not as strong.

The nurses were very quick to welcome you onto the ward, after asking who I was, then directed me to the main ward to where Amanda and Yvonne were. There were only 6 beds and just 4 were occupied, Yvonne was going to stay with Amanda and I having to be at work for 5 am in the morning I will have to commute every evening. It was not ideal but hey it is what it is, at least if I wanted to see them I am forced to accept arrangement or take time off work. Reluctantly I had to make my way home at 9 pm, Amanda was still fitting violently but doctors would be coming to see her hopefully in the next 15 minutes or so.

I arrived home to an empty cold house around 10.38 pm in the evening, before I could do anything my first job was to poke the fire and get some heat in the house. The fire was a Baxi-Boiler, and it took extraordinarily little time to heat the radiators and hot water tank in the roof, next I made a large mug of coffee before filling the bath. There is nothing like a soak in a hot bath to relax the stresses of the day, I even included half a jar of rose petal bath salts boy that smelt fabulous and clearly permeated though out the bungalow.

I eventually managed to get to bed at one thirty in the morning, the alarm clock which was so loud and sounded like a fire bell woke me with a start. I again, did the wrong thing of switching it off and have that extra five minutes or so, I wish I had not I must have fallen back into a deep sleep only to find when I woke the so called five minutes turned out to be two hours. Well that certainly felt sickening and the day has only just started, it was pointless hurrying now, I went into the kitchen to make a coffee but found I had not finished drinking the one from last night. There was that horrible scum you get after coffee had gone stone cold after standing a long time. What is also left is a brown ring on the inside of the mug. It did not smell too good either a sickly smell of stale cigarettes come to mind, I even smelt the stale cigarette smoke on my work clothes and put them in the wash.

"I eventually rolled into work at about 11 am I reported to the shop floor supervisor and told her why I was late, she must have been in a stinking mood also. Her snappy attitude toward me I suppose was justified but totally in opinion out of order snapping at my workmates, I put it down to her time of month. She will notify personnel and I may be called to the office later to explain the reasons for being late to the Personnel officer. I'm pleased to say. That call never came, and I completed the work by the end of my shift. When I got home I rang the hospital to find out about Amanda how she was and to pass on to Yvonne that I would be over about 8 pm all being well.

I say all being well because the weather had changed instead of having a star-studded sky, a thick blanket of fog had arrived. Yvonne came to the phone and explained that Amanda had a bad night and was moved to a small single bed isolation room, she was all right, but felt she might upset other patients on the ward That was the sad news, the good news was since this morning Amanda has only had two hundred and twelve fits that was pleasing to hear. Yvonne also new about the weather forecast and suggested that I did not come over to Norwich as reports were saying it was in places quite thick, there was no way I was not going and told her I was bringing her sister Joyce over so I would not be on my own. I was unaware just how bad the weather was, Oulton Broad and Beccles the problem was the marsh mist it was quite an eerie sight and reminded me of Sherlock Holmes and the Moore scenes in the film "Hounds of the Baskervilles." The low intrusive mist caught headlights of the oncoming vehicles as they came toward you then disappear into oblivion to only then reappear in front of you in some way it was quite exhilarating and at the same time quite scary. It proved to be identical the other side of Beccles as we hit the main Norwich highway, there is of course many more hills and dales twists and turns to negotiate along the journey which at times proved rather hazardous but we made it safely to the hospital more I think with the divine intervention from the man above. Hopefully, the return journey will not be as bad a little naivety on my behalf don't you think?

We did make it home although much slower than going, I intend not to do that again, in a hurry that is a certainty "I can assure you." Our whole bodies we're shaking like a leaf, strange how fear acts on the human body. "Brrrrr!" I finished work just after 6 pm, after what can only describe as an interesting one and was really welcoming. There was a gas leak in the cold store department alarms were going off all over the factory, everyone stopped work turned off the machines and went to their own designated emergency staging areas. Naturally, the company employed their own emergency fire service, still the

Suffolk fire service and two ambulances arrived in less than four minutes the police department who are stationed about less than two minutes away took ten minutes to arrive. The problem was found quite quickly and dealt with, we were informed later in the day that there was a damage gas pipe which had to be replaced and after 50 minutes giving the smell of gas to clear were once more allowed back into the factory so production could resume.

I wasted no time in getting home ran a bath and made a coffee, I would have something to eat when I get back from the hospital. Unfortunately, I was not going to make it tonight, I only got around the corner when I was aware of burning plastic, the smell was toxic; smoke was coming from beneath the dashboard. I turned off the engine and scrambled out of the car expecting it suddenly to burst into flame or blow up, thankfully it did neither and proved to be from the internal fuse box disabling the car completely.

There was no way I would make it over tonight; I rang the hospital to inform them of my problem, I would telephone Yvonne tomorrow, and would they please pass on the message. Thankfully, it was a new switch I installed several weeks ago, one of the wires to the switch had parted and that caused an electrical short. The toxic smell had gone new fuses installed and things were back to normal, I telephone the hospital spoke to Yvonne who was having a break something to eat and drink before returning to Amanda's bedside.

Amanda had an unbelievably bad night her seizures were extraordinarily strong and the doctors have been struggling to control them. They are still unable to place a finger on the cause they have decided to transfer Amanda to Cambridge arrangements will be confirmed tomorrow, they would also be sending medical records too. She may be there obviously a few days or so hospital notes with a senior nurse as Yvonne was naturally going with Amanda, it was therefore pointless me coming over until they return, she would call me when they get back to Norfolk and Norwich.

As it was almost the weekend it would not be till Monday at the earliest that consultant paediatricians would see Amanda, then and only then would they decide what investigations. If anything could be worth doing, "my thoughts and fears are they may just be going through the motions!" I truly hope I am wrong I do not know who we can go to next, the one thing we do know is will never ever let Amanda down and shall continue to fight her corner till the end of time itself. Yvonne informed me that Amanda has so far today had 162 making the total of I know it to be more but to err on the side of probability there certainly exclude those seizures we did not see after leaving the hospital or when she attended tests. "How long can her frail body take this please if God is out there again, we pray you're healing hand is desperately needed."

Amanda remained in Norfolk and Norwich for about several weeks in that time they had run many tests, in fact the same tests she had when in Gt. Yarmouth. I think that may have been our second opinion, how stupid is that I ask you. They did change her anti-convulsant medication and she is now taking Epanutin, I understand it is slightly stronger than Epilim, the seizures I am pleased to say have dramatically changed in both severity and numbers. None of which are related to the change in her medication, the decoration work to the Great. Yarmouth hospital is done, and Amanda will be transferred back either tomorrow or Monday.

It is my guess Monday will be moving day I am not infallible just like you I am a mortal human being and unbelievably have been known to get things wrong occasionally, but we will see I feel lucky. I had to see my GP today and ask if I could have a medical note as I am mentally drained from the travelling back and forth to Norwich every day not getting home till late at night and having to be in work for five thirty in the morning then having to do a twelve-hour shift dashing home changing and then making my way over to Norwich is beginning to take its toll on me.

Dr Aylwood did not even hesitate and signed me off for a fortnight, if I required a further certificate, I only had to phone the surgery. "Well would you believe it; I'll go to the bottom of the stairs. or I would if I had stairs as we live in a bungalow. Amanda was not being transferred until next week" Not to worry I am off work so there will be no hurry in traveling back and forth to Norwich, Yvonne must at times feel quite lonely not seeing a friendly face or two. The pressure and worries we have had to endure and live with have dramatically lightened, Amanda's had very few seizures over the past few days and the one's she has had are Known as petti mal basically twitching which lasted a matter of seconds.

Before the twitching started Amanda seemed as if in a trance a state much like a floppy rag doll and lasting only seconds if one were not aware of it happening would I'm sure certainly have miss it, we both watched Amanda very closely. Yvonne and I do not want to return to those nasty grand mal seizures she had been having, and now has a chance to re-build the strength she lost over the past couple of months. We were soon back in Yarmouth hospital the smell of freshly painted walls and ceilings hit as we climbed the stairs, signs placed on the ward walls recommending everyone to be careful just in case the door frames were still wet the last thing, anyone wanted was for visitors going home covered with paint marks on their clothes.

Amanda was sleeping quite soundly not a single sign of a seizure or twitch all day. Last night Yvonne was able to feed Amanda and at lunchtime she managed to eat a whole jar of "Cow & Gate" Lamb with vegetables, followed by half a jar of Cherry desert. We quietly placed her in her cot and covered her with just a sheet as it was on the warm side, hopefully she will wake for her tea before we leave. Yvonne looked tired and was looking forward to her own bed, the night nurses were waking her throughout the night to feed Amanda and she had to use a breast pump to extract her milk which she informed me was worse than tooth ache. Yvonne is someone who loves her sleep and becomes quite moody if she must get up early, having children getting up for work in the morning was a nightmare but once up she would take an hour to come fully humanised if that is a word I can use. Amanda did wake before we left for home, she drank half a bottle of warmed milk and the promptly gave some back as we winded her. The night staff have her rostered for two hourly feeds: all bottles have been prepared and in the fridge, all that needs to be done is to warm them up.

Amanda appeared relaxed and fast asleep and as it was "Nine thirty we said our good-byes," We were going to be in early tomorrow as it was the doctor's round and doctor. Back was going to be there; we have not seen him in almost three weeks so there are questions to be asked and I hope he has some answers. Well, we are now well into November and still we have no idea of the cause of Amanda's illness, she has been poked, prodded, and pulled about they have stuck needles into her head arms hands feet blood test after blood tests and still found nothing. I made this observation and recorded them in a daily diary, any statements made in this diary are factual and will be used at some point in the future.

Our feelings and conclusions over the past months have been one of anger, frustration, guilt, and disappointment in medical practitioners' failure in finding not a single cause or if they have, keeping it away from us. One blessing we have is Amanda still is free of gran- mal seizures allowing her in some way to build up strength, certainly stress is playing havoc with her little mind. Is the fact that we are now over the worst and unknowingly found the cause or are we about to see mega eruption never seen before ("calm before the storm springs to mind.")

Chapter Seven

TAKING AMANDA HOME

I t was not hard to comprehend the news we were given this morning when we arrived at the hospital, Amanda was going to be discharged today around two thirty this afternoon. Doctor. Back for the first time since Amanda had been an inpatient you seem to have become more humanised, a look of pleasure on his face his hair was brushed back showing a receding hairline new deep brown shoes shirt and tie made me a little uneasy. Even his posture had changed he had become more upright instead of having shoulders depressingly bent forward causing him to almost shuffle, it might also have contributed to his ogre type persona.

Amanda had greatly improved; the level of anti-convulsant appears at last taken effect, strangely they still have failed to find the reasons behind her illness, the outcome of seeing Amanda seizure free for the time being our frustration and annoyance to the fact we remain in the dark as to the cause. Doctor. Back is quite happy to allow her home for her very first Christmas, Yvonne, and I were as you can imagine over the moon our hearts were pounding with excitement it has been almost four whole months in hospital being poked prodded and underwent tests of every description.

The Nursing staff were emotionally excited and relieved that Amanda was going home, at Times while in their care they were drawn deeply to tears and were forced to watch helplessly unable to comfort her or take away the pain she must be enduring. If the truth been known, we had doubted this day would ever come. The Nursing Staff also were emotionally relieved, Amanda had changed over the past five months now well and truly behind us, and that's where it should stay. Before leaving we presented the nurses with a large box of chocolates and a thank you Card, it was nearly three thirty in the afternoon.

We had a wonderful Christmas the problems we met over the last Five months are now outdated; we had all the family around us. Yvonne's mum, dad, her sisters Joan, Joyce, and Carolyne my mum my Stepfather Alex and Anne-Marie. There were aunt's uncle's niece's nephews. from Wales, brother's sister's family members from Liverpool all having made. the long journey to Lowestoft. How Yvonne's parents found the room to accommodate them all was a miracle, but they managed it. The Hazelwood family were renowned for their parties at Christmas and the New Year, the residents of Southfield Gardens would join in with the revelry and madness as the festive ramblings spilled unselfishly onto the street. The best moments apart from the Christmas singing was the New Year's conga we tried to include everyone, knocking on doors all down one side of Southfield Gardens then up the other no one was left out. This certainly proved to be for us one of the happiest times we as a family have had over the last four months, if only it could last forever like the USA's Groundhog celebrations. The festive season passed by very quickly and the new year came in with a bang, temperatures. dropped frost appeared thick on the ground starting off the day.

An eerie low mist covered the ground, grass, bushes, twigs, and even the final remaining dead brown leaves from trees did not escape the frost and became covered with Icey particles which crunched as you stood on them. It was so cold it made ones breathe to be seen, fingers would turn almost white your ears nose and cheeks would turn red and finally, this was made worse by the biting cold wind that accompanied it.

Yvonne Anne marie, Amanda and I were certainly not going to let the cold weather stop us from taking a walk around the block. After breakfast we wrapped Amanda up with warm blankets a woolly hat and a thermal pram cover, well this was when all said and done, her first taste of winter was it not? We would put on the kettle so the oldies could have a brew before getting out of bed, then it was into the front room to light the gas fire keeping the doors shut to keep in the heat.

Amanda fell asleep as we left the house and remained so for the whole time, we were out, every time stopped she would stir and when we moved on, she again, settled down this continued to occur every time she was taken out for a walk. Yvonne and I had not realised just how cold it was outside as we were wrapped up to the nines, the temperature while we were out had dropped dramatically. Our fingers were bluish in colour and felt as if they were burning our noses so cold, they began dripping, I was glad I had a hanky in my pocket at least Amanda was as warm as toast, so, we made for home after about thirty minutes or so. Never were we so pleased to hold a mug of tea in our numb hands even though it proved a little difficult at first, little did we know but our lives were to change once again dramatically. Amanda has become quite restless and crying almost constantly, nothing we did could pacify her she would not eat or drink anything. We decided not to hang about and took her to see her GP Dr. Van Pelt, he advised us to take her over to the hospital and would call ahead to notify them of our coming.

On arrival Amanda was examined firstly by the Nursing staff and then again, by a very young-looking paediatric doctor by the name of doctor. Dutter, she was from India and about thirty years of age not very tall about five feet eight inches in hight and dressed in a light blue sari, which was pulled over the head, then dropped loosely over her shoulders and seemed to be tied just below her bust, there was a gap around the waist which was bare. there in her belly button eyes were drawn to a deep red jewel and below that a mid-green wrap around skirt light brown sandal's which could only been seen as she walked. Her hair was jet black and for the fact her top covered her three foot long platted could been seen now and then when she moved down her back.

Yvonne and I were asked to get something to eat while doctor. Dutter examined her and read up on her notes, it would take about an hour or so. We were reluctant to go but we had to look after ourselves for Amanda's sake, the time flew by and we were gone just under two hours to find Amanda connected once more to an Intravenous Drip the nurses had also placed a nasal gastric tube down her nose. Doctor. Dutter had an urgent call to attend to and left instruction asking if we would mind waiting for her to return so she could have a chat about today. We naturally became quite anxious as we thought things were going well it was just this nasty cold, she had picked up, her constant crying and refusing any drink we tried to give her.

It was about Seven thirty when Dr Dutter returned, she was very apologetic and hoped we would stay as requested. She began by explaining the action she had taken regarding the IV and Nasal tubes while she was examining Amanda, she felt she was a little dehydrated and needed to get fluid into her hence the NG tube, her cold was quite nasty so, to give her a course of drugs she was given the IV. Dr Dutter could see how concerned we both were, she explained that Amanda was a new patient. She asked if we fully understood about Amanda's condition and if we had been kept up to date with everything appertaining to her illness, we had to admit there were many questions that had not been answered the main one being "why she is having major seizures and what is causing them?"

We were aware of numerous tests carried out Blood, urine eyes etc, but no real explanations on why these tests we're being carried out or being told of the outcome or findings of many of the results. It has been a daily question that spilt from our lips, only to be told we are waiting for the results to come back wewere always being given excuses on why results we're not available excuses such as they were late, lost, doctors unavailable to receive the results as they were away or they were inconclusive.

I would say the inconclusive excuse was the best one. The look on doctor. Dutter's face showed her disappointment and to some extent disgust that things had not been explained to us fully, "I'm sure Mr & Mrs Cherry, she said you are aware that Amanda is an extremely sick little girl!" "Searching for reasons of her illness is clearly not going be easy." She has presented us with several serious problems, what we have found so far is this Amanda suffering from the following medical problems.

- She is severely Brain Damaged; "how have we come to this prognosis.
- well, we have measured her head and has not grown for a child of her age.

- From test carried out on her eyes there is clearly no reaction to light.
- Her hearing is very acute to say the least, we have found that any sudden noise makes her jump out of her skin.
- Amanda is also showing signs of spasticity in her arms, legs, and body.
- Regular blood and urine tests confirm that both Amanda's kidneys are also damaged and will be closely monitored. Amanda's grand-mal seizure is baffling everyone, reasons at this moment in time is greatly eluding the Hospital medical Clinicians.
- With all those issues they have found Amanda is suffering from why can they not diagnose the reasons that cause her seizures.

I have asked on many occasions could these seizures have been due to the maternity unit forcing Yvonne to have a measles vaccination, they felt her immunity was on the low side. Before being given the booster, vaccine Yvonne became worried as she was intending to breast feed, reassurance from the medical clinician that having this would not harm the baby. One tends to believe those doctors know everything, we took him at his word; then three weeks later Amanda came down with a rash covering almost one hundred percent of her body. The frightening thing was as we watched it spread, we were physically unable to prevents the spread; the itching must have been chronic for Amanda. She had an elevated temperature and seemed to be burning up; a very loud high-pitched screaming had us panicking, we tried wrapping a cool wet towel around her in hope this might help reduce some of the itch. Yvonne and I watched as the rash began to vanish as quickly as it came, then her violent uncontrollable seizures started to what we are left with today.

Chapter Eight

IGNORANCE AT ITS WORST

Tests and more tests took place over the last two weeks and again no information was given regarding results, naturally we continued asking for information and we still got the same response echoing from their lips nothing to report at this stage still awaiting results from the labs. Amanda over the past few days began to look rather puffy especially around her facial cheeks, they also appeared a little blushed drawing our eyes to the problem. Amanda was also, back on an IV infusion and NG tube, Sister Jordan walked in and explained that Amanda had been fitting and the doctor on call had decided to put on a mild dose of steroids again they had also changed her drugs to try and control her seizures.

We were aware of the IV and NG being done though we were not told why until now, surely, we should have been notified about the drug change and to the fact they had given her steroid treatment. "Yet again we were being kept out of what was going on." I know I should not have taken my frustration out on the nursing staff, but like any front-line workers they are the first to cop the anger. I asked Sister Jordan If she could get the doctor here so that I can get anexplanation as to why we have not been consulted on the action taken, Yvonne and I need to nip this issue in the bud it cannot continue like this.

It was late in the afternoon when the doctor eventually arrived, by then I had calmed down enough to apologise to the ward staff and no damage was done, at least I hope not. He explained to us that Amanda had not been particularly good crying and twitching quite badly, he had prescribed Valium required and had also started a course of steroids to see if that might help reduce the seizures, she was having. Unfortunately, the prescribed steroids do not seem to be doing any good so we stopped the medication yesterday, as for her drug change yes, we have changed it but only on the dosage strength that has changed and will naturally be reviewed by doctor. Back next week.

Yvonne and I arrived early at the hospital today only because Amanda had been again, rather poorly, she has changed completely overnight, and her seizures are increased dramatically in both strength and in number. As we climbed the steps to the ward there was a pungent aroma emanating from the ward, the closer we got to the top of the steps the stronger it became. An aroma not very pleasant at first as it seemed to bring on a headache till you became used to it, it had a slight burning sensation in your mouth not to un-pleasant in fact how can I describe it…. Not that dissimilar from sucking on a Trebor Extra Strong Mint.

The aroma also penetrated our clothes which we could only smell when we left the ward to get something to eat at lunchtime, clearly our taste buds were problematic as nothing we ate or drank had any effect of clearing and remained on our taste buds for the rest of the day. Sister Jordan must have seen us arrive and walked in before we had the chance to remove our coats, she informed us that last night Amanda was ill her seizures this time were the worst they had ever seen. Doctors struggled to try and prevent them but had not option open to them but to physically sedate her, they prescribe a drug called "Paraldehyde." Sister Jorden explained that this drug although a rather nasty drug is only used when it is necessary and has some serious side effects, being a thick oil-based drug and thick in substance can only be administered either intramuscularly with a glass syringe and large thick needle, or it can be given to a patient via their rectum neither way is pleasant for the patient as this way it causes the rectum to suffer a burning sensation like severe nappy rash and we all know what that is like.

If it must be given continually by needle into the muscular tissues, it can eventually cause serious and permanent muscle damage, it made us cringe. Doctor. Back eventually made an appearance his glasses perched on his head. He spent a brief time reading Amanda's medical notes and asking Sister Jordan on Amanda's status over the last 12 hours, as she was speaking, he began examining Amanda starting with her feet pulling her legs stretching twisting and the same with Amanda's arms. "Puzzled" by what I was witnessing I had to ask the question, "why he felt it necessary to pull her about in that manner and what information did he gain from it if anything at all?" His answer "it among other things showed me how supple her joints are and if there is a problem with joints etc" Doctor Back she is so sedated your actions are in this case, pointless, as she does not have the ability to protest or resist.

It has now been a total of 5 months that Amanda has been under you, can you please tell us if you have managed to find the cause of her 1,178, 280 seizures and yes you heard me right, and they Doctor are only the ones we have physically witnessed. You have carried out phenomenal number of tests from skin biopsies and allergy samples a numerous plethora of daily blood tests including EEG's, ECG's and finally Lumber Punctures at least as far as I know 3 of those. "So, doctor. Back, what is the cause of Amanda's condition"? His response again was a negative one, Amanda is showing so many symptoms no one cause can be identified.

I could feel the knots building in my stomach, my heart was beginning to thump louder and louder in my head. Frustration and anger increasing every time he gave this pathetic excuse, surely Dr Back if you are unable to find what the trouble is then it is time you have Amanda sent to a hospital that has the technology and equipment surely to find that needle in a haystack. "Mr. Cherry!" tests of which I agree have been many, have so far not yielded any positive results we have still a few outstanding results that have so far not been sent back, "fine"! so what that tells me Doctor. Back and I do say this with a touch of sarcasm in my voice all those tests you sent away I would allege confirms your own findings which eludes my human intelligence as why the results have not been shared with us Amanda's Parents.

Clearly Amanda's condition was frustrating him for answers as much as they we're frustrating Yvonne and me, but as I continued to remind myself, he is after all, just a qualified Professor of Tropical Diseases. Amanda remained in a comatose state for the rest of the day, although we were not wishing this to last too long at least for the time being her little heart was relaxing and able to regain a little strength since the beginning of this awesome illness. It also gave me the opportunity to catch up on her daily diary, "Yep" in all the commotions of the past few months, I have been keeping a written record in diary form of everything that is happening with Amanda.

The idea behind that is so I can look back on how she has been the days when she has been unwell, how many seizures she has had while we have been with her. The feeding habits and how Amanda has coped with oral or NG tube feedings, what doctors have done or not done. Drugs changes we are made aware of tests carried out when doctors decide to inform us about, Questions put to the doctors and the answers that were given in response you name it I assure you it will be recorded Amanda is our daughter and however much hospital medical practitioners may feel it out of order, we will always be there to fight Amanda's corner.

Today I have quite a report to write up and now we have been made aware of failure in the reporting of test outcomes and are still waiting for results, tests we now understand were carried out in the past few days. Every time I put pen to paper my emotions get the better of me, it is just so difficult to come to terms with the fact our hands are tied and there is nothing we can do to help. Sister Jordan has informed us that Amanda is to be woken up from her sedation and it is hoped that the seizures will have subsided, it has been an anxious few days, but it has enabled some rest bite but at a cost to Amanda's bottom which is looking very sore from the burning Paraldehyde oil. Naturally, we have been covering the area with cooling cream, but still, it is looking incredibly angry.

We are now into April Amanda has been in hospital for almost three months give or take a couple of days and still the hospital has not discovered the reason for her condition. In fact, it has become a regular daily question we put to the medical practitioners, like a broken record the answers are the same and the response back is the same. If you cannot find out why from all the tests, then send her to another hospital that may have the technology and machinery to look.

Doctor. Back was on his regular ward rounds I again challenge him to send Amanda to another hospital and to see if they have better success than Gt. Yarmouth, it had just past two o'clock on Friday 25th April 1980. I explicitly recall both the time and date because as I persisted in asking if a cause had been found, for the first time ever in my questioning he totally lost it…. "MR CHERRY"! …. "How many times must I remind you Amanda has been to Cambridge, to the Norfolk and Norwich Hospitals and they were unable to find a cause."

"DOCTOR. BACK!" please; you insult my intelligence" by now my patience was really being tested, "doctor. Back"! for fear of repeating myself Amanda was only sent to Norfolk and Norwich Hospital because you we're having this ward painted." "As for sending her to Cambridge; it is in my opinion to cover your back and recheck your investigations and results." It is also my belief that in my opinion you and you alone want to find the answers no matter what the cost to patient or family, and why do I allege this; well; allow me to explain.

May I remind you doctor Back the first day we brought Amanda into this hospital, you called me in to your office and your actual words to me were and I quote "Amanda was a sick child and I suggest it would be in her best for you to leave Amanda here go home and forget you ever had her"!!!... "What were you're intensions doctor? "Were your intensions Dr" to treat her as a Lab rat to experiment on…" "Well…."? You have no idea; just hearing that suggestion, you made to "**Leave her here and forget that we had her**"! My wife carried this gift from God for nine months suffering morning sickness and as the months progressed; and the baby grew, restless nights as the baby kicked and turned. What God given right have you to decide what we should or should not do that is God's decision and Gods alone, hearing this coming out of your mouth I wanted to knock you clean through the small windows in your office.

The day proved to be another lengthy one for all concerned, Amanda's seizures although only pettimal were so numerous today (407) it hurts us so much our anger and frustration seemed to be lost somehow in the minds of the clinicians. There in that hospital cot lay a little girl hooked up to tubes and wires, what must be going through her little mind we will never know. As our visit came ever nearer to its close, we recorded the number of seizures Amanda has had to so far today as 407, increasing her overall total recorded to a massive 1,178, 280 Amanda was given her medication at 8 pm still without any answers to our questions. We have had an exceptional tiring day tackling the so, called medical practitioners again without answers, Yvonne, and I decided we would leave for home.

We needed to collect Anne-Marie from her nannies it has been two days since we last saw her; our time has selfishly been spent trying to sort Amanda's problems and therefore we have wrongly pushed Anne-Marie away. It was pointed out that Anne-Marie had needs; one being the ability to see her mum and dad, according to her nanny she felt she was missing hugs and kisses she was hurting just as much she found it hard to understand what was wrong with her sister.

We decided that we must sit down with Anne-Marie and take time to explain why her sister has spent so much time in hospital, but it is hard to explain fully the problem especially as we are ourselves not fully privy to all the answers. I suppose Yvonne and I are greatly worried as to how much Anne-Marie can handle and understand, she might have only been eight and a half; but she had a grown-up head on her shoulders and like me at her age had to grow up quickly and I will always be so proud of her.

The day ended disappointingly we were going to get soaked going to the car, not only was it hammering down with rain, but we were bang in the centre of a major thunderstorm fork lightning that lit up the heavens. As we reached the car there was a massive bang so loud I swear it created a shockwave, somewhere close by must have been hit as it blew out the streetlights including the lights in in the hospital and houses around the area. The hospital has a large generator of some kind as the blackout was truly short lived, even so the Blackness was quite frightening especially as we were suddenly plunged into complete darkness and you realise just how much we take for granted when it comes down to our need for streetlights.

Chapter Nine

STARTED ANOTHER NEW DRUG

Today Yvonne and I were a little late arriving at the hospital, the storm of last night kept us up till around three o'clock in the morning. Listening to the early morning news on the radio it was reported that a house close to the beach had been struck and severely damaged it must be pulled down and rebuilt. That explains why we so clearly felt a shockwave as the house was apparently only two streets from the hospital how frightening is that, at least there were no injuries or loss of life as the owners we understand were visiting their daughter in Oxford but what a thing to come home to.

Amanda had another bad night, and the doctor was called in to see her, it was decided that it might be prudent to try another anti-convulsant drug. What we found out later was that the drug is from the same family as Epilim which she has now been taken off, they have now replaced it with Epanutin which doctors say has worked successfully better on patients who suffer from epilepsy and is a slightly stronger in its dosage. We were told that it will take a little while before we see some positive results; I asked how long a little while is? The doctors think that it would certainly be no more than two to three days at the most, it is hard to say with Amanda but at least by the weekend. In fact, the drug took forty-eight hours to get to work. We were so astonished when we came in to find that Amanda's seizures had somewhat reduced in strength and consistency, but we could not become too excited as Amanda has proven to be stubborn child and does quite the opposite to what one would expect. This hospital admittance continued for the next three weeks and her seizure count for this time was more than 518, bringing the total to 1,178,798 again I must confirm these are the figures that Yvonne and I have personally witnessed and reported in her diary. We are not sure if the new Epanutin medication they have put Amanda on is working, at least we can see little visible evidence to warrant us to become excited about. It was almost ten 'clock in the evening Amanda was about to have her medication and two hundred mls of milk through her NG tube, it seemed quite late but to be fair the nurses had been remarkably busy since they took over from the afternoon staff at 7 pm. Amanda was fitting intensely and the noise she was making was quite alarming, clearly Amanda was not only in distress, but this confirmed she was almost certainly, in some pain.

As usual we were rather reluctant to leave when Amanda was like this, but the nursing staff assured us they would call us if needed but they never did. On the way home we stopped at our favourite chip shop and bought our usual half chicken and chips each, we will begin to look like a chicken at this rate but they were to die for. We were now at our wits end with Doctor Back and his paediatric team they continue to ignore our desperate requests to send Amanda to another hospital, allowing them to carryout independent examinations who can say; with a fresh pair of eyes and attacking the problem might discover something new? Over the last four days the total number of seizures count reach another staggering total of 1332, bringing the total to 1,1890 130. Both Yvonne and I feel enough is enough they have had their chance to find the reasons behind Amanda's Seizures and gain some success in controlling them. We could take no more Amanda was going like the clappers and we asked the doctor Back be called, it was well over three hours before he made an appearance only to let us know how inconvenient it was to pull him away from a social evening, he had been attending. "Tuff titty!" I screamed back, Yvonne and I have been here since seven thirty this morning and in all the time we have had a junior doctor on his staff show his face and prescribe Amanda be given a rectal Valium and he would inform doctor Back when next he's able to make contact.

Well doctor Back I formally notify you verbally and in front of the ward Sister "THIS IS NOT GOOD ENOUGH," social event or no social event. Amanda is not as we have said before on many occasions a "LAB RAT" for you to experiment on, you have failed our child dramatically either you have Amanda transferred to a hospital like Great Ormond Street in London, or I will remove her personally myself. Take her to London and then seek advice from a solicitor on how I can take this further, naturally I would not or could not remove her in the state she was in, but he did not know that I was so angry I think it convinced him to go away and take my threat seriously. After months of shouting and pushing our request have been accepted, Amanda is to betransferred too Great Ormond Street Hospital.

Arrangements ambulance with escort would take her on Monday morning, unfortunately, if I wanted to go, I would have to follow behind the Ambulance in my car. I am not too happy with that idea as they do not exactly hang around and as I do not know where the hospital is in London if I lose the ambulance, I will have to return home. Strange how in a second things can change decisions are altered for the good. Sister Jordan walked on the ward and said we have a Mr Robert Barker who intends to visit his son in Great Ormond Street and cannot get a train, would I consider taking him as he knows the way; well, I was not going to turn an offer like that so not hesitating I immediately agreed. The feeling of sheer gratifying relief ran through my body the adrenalin relaxed in fact I had been so worried that I became quite tiered physically, Mr Barker came onto the ward: a man in I would say in his early forties clean shaven and fair coloured hair.

We got talking as one does and told me about his two-year-old son who was undergoing a major operation on his heart, he was separated from his estranged wife for some three years and he had won the full custardy of his son Andrew. Robert like me seemed emotionally drained and this showed when talking about the events that had happened in his personal life, the exceedingly difficult lengthy divorce proceedings from his wife coupled with that the serious illness of Andrew clearly had taken its toll.

Robert and I just seemed to click with each other, and I certainly hoped we can continue as friends anyway. The ability to discuss issues of a similar elk can in my opinion I believe at lighten the trouble effecting one's heart. The door opened and in walked Sister Jordan carrying a tray "Coffee!" "Oh! thank you, Sister we were feeling rather dry, oh and chocolate biscuits you are pushing the boat out" we could not help but laugh. "don't think for one moment I intend making this a habit." If I did not know Sister Jordan as well as I did, I would certainly, have thought she meant it.

Still, we had really settled down and arrange the travel pick up points and time for Monday, not that there was any need for lengthy negotiation required. Meet here at seven thirty cups of coffee load the Ambulance and follow behind, great done and dusted and continued drinking our coffee and eating those fantastic chocolate biscuits ha! ha! A doctor walked in to examine Amanda he wrote up another prescription of drugs including more rectal Valium, again as usual Yvonne applied some "SUDACREAME" to her bottom and the rawness was unbelievable it was as red as the skin of a ripened tomato that must be so painful certainly, I think is a major factor to her crying.

The time was now close to 7.30 pm before we left for home, we could tube feed her, what we were not expecting was Sister Jordon suggesting we replace the NG tube ourselves, we were very reluctant to do that in case we got it wrong. She was confident we could do it and said she will watch and tell us how, what and if we would be doing it wrong. So being the coward I was, I let Yvonne have the pleasure of going first. It looked certainly easier than I imagined, and Amanda did not gag once, to check the tube was in the correct place i.e., the stomach Yvonne was given a syringe to draw up some bile from her stomach confirming that she had done it correctly well done darling! She was so proud of her achievement I am reminded of it constantly, it certainly was not easy as it looked. Amanda was fitting quite badly but not to worry it will be my turn at some point and I will have to make sure I do not mess up.

Amanda bathed changed and fed had her drugs and figuratively settled down for the night, Amanda was fitting like there was not a tomorrow 180 in total we have counted so far. Not only effects the guilt we both had leaving her, the uneasiness entering our minds; wary about being called back either as we descend the stone stairwell or after we got home. That feeling is constantly with us and one might say we would be used to it, maybe they should experience the trauma it certainly would open their eyes to the ruthless reality of it all.

As we turned the key in the lock the fear we felt as the telephone was ringing there was a life reality check our hearts almost stopped as I dashed into the bedroom to answer it "Hello!" I felt a sigh of relief as the voice on the other end said its mum. "How are things with Amanda today"? I decided to hand the telephone over to Yvonne as I knew it was not going to be a particularly short call, I went into the kitchen an made a hot sugary drink. The phone call lasted over an hour but it also included talking to Anne-Marie and keeping her up to date with her sister's illness, we promised to take her to see her over the weekend as Amanda would be going to London.

Anne-Marie was extremely excited today as she was going to see her little sister, it was quite difficult to calm her and kept asking if we can go now. Yvonne insisted that before we go anywhere, we must have some breakfast and a cup of tea and coffee. If only Anne-Marie was as eager and excited at getting up on a school day a miracle I know but we can dream.

It was quite windy this morning but at least it was dry, it took us longer to get to the hospital today due to the fact a trustee prisoner had absconded from Blunderston Prison while out working in the fields. Rather making a joke of the wording of "(Trustee)," anyway there were Police roadblocks in place for almost two miles along dual carriageway to Gt. Yarmouth checking vehicles leaving Lowestoft going North.

Arriving at the hospital Anne-Marie literally ran up the tower steps, at one-point stumbling as her foot slipped on one of the smooth steps. Turning to see how far we were behind her she called out to us to hurry up, the gate placed at the top of the steps we knew would be locked and naturally meant she would have to wait till we caught her up. The wards night sister met us at the top of the stairwell to open the gate, "Amanda has had quite a nasty night and they had to call the duty paediatrician out and she was in with Amanda working on her. (It was not till later we were told what working on Amanda meant), for the last two hours Amanda stopped breathing three times.

Each time the doctor struggled to resuscitate her; Amanda has now been stabilised but to be on the safe side she has been sedated; there is an oxygen mask laying near her face, the drip in her arms must have been difficult to put in as her little hand was looking quite swollen and instead of being supported by a see-through plaster a bandaged covered her arm to her elbow. Naturally, this was the last thing we wanted to do was to bring Anne-Marie and to see her sister suffering, we were both surprised at the way Anne-Marie handled the whole issue and if deep down she was frightened by what she saw or did an excellent job of not showing it at her early age.

Boy it has made both of us so proud of her, she is certainly handling Amanda's illness better than her, me, or her mum. It was going to be sometime before we would be able to see Amanda, the doctor was hanging around just in case Amanda again, stops breathing. I am not too sure that the doctor had been qualified for many years as she became a little agitated at our presence to begin with. I wonder if the struggle she had with Amanda frightened her a bit I know if it were me, I would be and if so, she would require emergency resuscitation. I am quite sure the ward nurses would be capable of handling that.

The fear I had was to take ourselves out of the picture, it was pointless being there at the time as Amanda had been deeply sedated. We thought we would get something to eat and then take

Anne-Marie to the pleasure beach for a couple of hours, she enjoyed herself on the kiddie's round-a-bout rides, penny slot machines, ice cream and candy floss even had a go on the water flume ended up getting soaked to the skin I will not be doing that again in a hurry I can tell you.

We finally took a horse and carriage ride along the sea front, which was an experience to behold Our nostrils were impregnated with the strong pungent smell of horse dung and wee, they did a lot of weeing I can confirm and only while they stood at the rank waiting for the next hire. Still, whatever was taken in at one end, was guaranteed to re-appear sometime later out the back. I assure you there was tons of it not just from one horse I might add, but eight of them tethered along the side of the road one behind the other. Not included were the four-spare relief horses that were tethered some twelve feet away doing the same thing. Picture this if you can as you are walking along Gt. Yarmouth Sea front, there in front of you stood several horses each chewing away on whatever they are fed on out of a nose bag strapped around its head a large bucket with water in front of it thick long rope attached to the bridal strap and at the other end, a heavy weight restraining it from bolting as cars passed remarkably close pass them.

Every horse was harnessed to a marvellous looking open top carriage with I would describe as floating springs, in other words whatever side you climbed into the carriage it would lean that way making it rock and sway as you got in most had little doors but not the one, we were in. Two colours black or mid brown, the seats were either red or brown which enhanced greatly the appearance and the driver was frantically polishing the body with a cloth to make everything glisten in the sun light.

The driver's seat was quite high about eighteen inches higher than the actual carriage itself a small metal clip loosely held his whip when not in use, behind the carriage hung another bucket this was I would think for the dung to be put as they cleaned up. The large amount of dung collected no doubt ensured the towns flower beds received its own quota of manure. The smell was so strong it even clung to our clothes, not really a wonderful thing to walk onto a hospital strongly smelling like a horse, at least everyone knew where we had spent our time.

Arriving back on the ward the young doctor had gone, Amanda remained sedated the look on the faces of the nursing staff said it all and we decided that we would go home have a bath change our smelly clothes and have some tea. We informed the staff we would return tomorrow smelling more like sweet roses, it raised a chuckle from everyone. We called in on the fish & Chip shop on the way home, Anne-Marie had cod and chips Yvonne had skate and chips I had steak and Kidney Pie with chips. The chippy thankfully was situated at the top of Kirkley Run less than two minutes from our front door, I cannot say we were not hungry, but it did not take us long to devour our full plates.

After our baths, a cup of tea and coffee we felt so tiered we went to bed at nine thirty, Anne-Marie fell asleep ten minutes after eating her tea. It did not feel that we had been asleep long as the alarm clock woke us up at seven, the bed was so warm and inviting I just wanted to turnover and remain tucked up for a few hours more but no way was that happening we had to get over to the hospital. We had a fry up; well egg and bacon sandwich with marmalade all though I say it myself this is a sandwich to die for believe me, a cup of tea and a mug of sweet coffee I was set to take Anne-Marie round to her nanny.

Sister Jordan was at Amanda's cot-side down and feeding her some milk, "Amanda had a quiet night" but naturally that can only be put down to her sedation. Apparently, doctors we're keeping a close watch on her and checked on her several times throughout the night just in case there was a repercussion of what happened in the early hours of yesterday morning. I asked Sister Jordan if tomorrow's trip to London would be cancelled because of the episode yesterday morning, "No" she said Amanda is expected and would be leaving at about ten o'clock in the morning. There will be an escort with her and for the journey down there Amanda will be in an incubator, I understand this is a common thing that happens with small children like Amanda. After a further recount of seizures I discovered that another 1,219 had been tucked between two pages of the diary, giving the true up to date total of seizures as 1,181,529.

Chapter Ten

AT LONG LAST GREAT ORMOND STREET HOSPITAL

As we sat having a coffee and tea, we both looked at each other, nothing strange about that one might say but we both had that puzzled look. Today the journey is a prayer both Yvonne and I have prayed for, and thought would never happen, to be able to have Amanda transferred from Gt. Yarmouth hospital to London's Gt. Ormond Street Hospital for sick Children.

For over three months now we have been arguing with clinicians (Dr. Back mostly), to send Amanda to a better equipped hospital and medical clinicians trained in Paediatric medicine to undertake their own investigations as to the cause of Amanda's condition. Now just an hour or so's time our prayers have been answered, yet here we are just about to challenge our own minds by worrying, have we possibly created a logistical problem.

Amanda has been hooked up to a heart monitor, intravenous drips, God knows what else to make this journey happen. The Ambulance arrived fifteen minutes late due to an accident on south town road involving a motorbike rider and a red car pulling out of a side road, anyway the Ambulance crew with the ward staff prepared Amanda for the journey. The Staff nurse on duty placed Amanda's medical notes at the bottom of her cot, she was given her medication and placed inside glass incubator like container. They had to unscrew the IV's and pass the screw end through the incubator's arm holes and reconnect them together again, that took almost five minutes and when they had done the checks, we made our way down to the Ambulance.

All that was left to do was to get into my car and to follow the Ambulance, Robert was waiting for me inside the car. "Boy" am I relieved Robert was with me, we literally lost the Ambulance as we were arriving at Wrentham. I have no idea what speed the driver was doing but as much to say I was certainly not going slow myself, well sixty-five; seventy tops at times the steering wheel was shaking and Robert suggested that might be due to the balance of my wheels being out they'll to be corrected urgently when I get back.

We eventually did catch up with the Ambulance just as we were driving into Gt. Ormond Street hospital, "Wow!" what a hospital, it was so, so Overwhelming. "Nothing at all like what I had a mental vision of" in fact literally the opposite, I had quite a shock as I entered the car parking area as we were stopped by the security guard as he lowered the barrier, "Sorry Sir" he said but you cannot come in with your car. I explained that I had just travelled from Lowestoft chasing the Ambulance that you just allowed through it was carrying my daughter who is seriously ill.

I was eventually allowed in and told where to park, he also informed me that I must find a car park outside the hospital as soon as possible. "Luckily," I found a space and reversed into it only to see it was reserved for one of the hospital doctors (tough) is my response: "Sometimes" one needs to do what one needs to do, and for me that time has arrived!

The delay by that obnoxious security guard had greatly caused us some time as Amanda had been taken into the admissions block and taken to the ward before we could get to her, not all was lost thank God the ambulance crew informed them we were coming so, a nurse hung back till we booked in. Not only was I breathless from running but I was shaking like a leaf, the adrenalin rushing through my body was making me feel quite sick so, the nurse arranged for us to be given a sugary Coffee as we were taken on the ward and introduced to the ward sister.

I thanked Robert and said we'll see each other later, he was off to his son Andrew and I hope he is well. Yvonne and I were both taken into an office where it was explained Amanda was being processed, while that was happening we had been allocated a guest room in the annex for both. We were advised to take out cases to the room and freshen up, by then the paediatricians looking after Amanda can ask questions about us and how much we know what has been done, confirm in their minds where to go from here.

It was quite a long walk, taking us into the bowels of the hospital, but we made it safely guided by a young nurse. She was rather on the slim about five-foot eight blond hair held back in a ponytail with a black hairband, a neat nurses cap was pinned with hairclips to prevent the cap from falling off. Even over here that clinical smell followed you around, I had extraordinarily little un-packing to do as I was not aware there would be a room for both of us. Before going back to the ward Yvonne and I were able to make ourselves a drink and the stress of the chase to London ease quite considerably, back on the ward we asked to explain Amanda's problem from the start our knowledge was rather intense and at times we had to keep going Over and over the same old statements. It almost felt that according to the questions to us were rather contradictory to what had been said in Amanda's medical, records laid on the table in front of us. Naturally, we both felt some uneasiness and that feeling was certainly being visible in both our voices, but more so I think in our body language. I am perched on the edge of the seat, biting on my bottom lip as my left leg is bobbing up and down this kind of gave it away don't you think?

It was only after the doctors finished their questioning that the sound of children on the ward, IV drip pumps bleeping and trollies squeaking wheels as they made their way across the highly polished floor which had been sprayed with a none slip coating making each step you made sound like you had stuck to the floor. Amanda had been booked to have many investigative test over the next seven days, scans MRI's a plethora of large blood tests and in-depth examinations and was one of the requests we made to the doctors at the meeting.

It was imperative the consultants be allowed to carry out an independent Examination even though it might mean having to repeat many of the examinations and test done at Gt. Yarmouth, hopefully their testing might find something missed and brought us close to concluding a more positive outcome different from that of Gt. Yarmouth Hospitals inconclusive findings. It was suggested from certain quarters of the medical profession as just "a stab in the dark" putting Amanda through unnecessary and in some cases painful testing and for what?

Comments like that are critically hurtful we are desperately trying as parents to find out why Amanda's violent grand-mal seizures cannot be controlled and find out if possible and most important

of all what has caused them there must be an answer.?
So, to those critics in the medical profession, it feels
in some way that you are seriously disappointed. All
who have had Amanda as their patient and worked on
Amanda over the months and failed to resolve issues
surrounding Amanda's condition we certainly feel
no animosity, and through no fault of your own, we
understand your hands were tied by the consultant
in charge.

Amanda was still having grand-mal seizures
and there were two doctors writing down not only
their observations, but also, I think recording the
length and strength of each seizure un-remarkably
similar to what was done in Gt. Yarmouth. There
really was nothing either Yvonne or I could do while
this was happening, and the ward sister Sally Rogers
approach us and told us that it might be beneficial if
we both went to the canteen and had something to
eat, she handed us both a meal voucher and said that
we would be given a proper pass tomorrow.

The canteen was surprisingly quite a walk from
the ward, and boy it was massive but the aroma
traveling down the corridor got one's juices working
overtime. On the menu tonight was quite a selection
Curry & Rice, Fish & Chips with mushy peas, Roast
Pork pea's Yorkshire puddings the size of small saucers

carrots mashed potato roast potato swede cabbage lovely thick gravy with other sauce condiments. For sweet there was a choice of Apple Pie with custard/cream, meringue jelly & Ice-cream there was so much of it our eyes almost popped out of there sockets.

The canteen was literally filled with doctors, nurses, parents of children who were in hospital for all types of conditions. Well, it is one of the world's leading authority on Child ailments and world's most famous hospital experience in the medical care of sick children. As we looked for a table to sit on my eyes were drawn to someone waving frantically it was Robert he had a couple of seats saved for us, "hello!" I said, fancy meeting you here! we all kind of chuckled as we saw the funny side.

After we had all eaten Robert suggested we might like to take a stroll along the Thames riverbank, Robert assured us it was not far from the hospital. "Why not" and with that we decided to pop quickly to the ward and let them know we were going to stroll along the riverbank and would be back in about an hour or so. It was going to be quite exciting for both Yvonne and me as the last time we visited London was on our Honeymoon, and that was just an overnight stay in the "Strand Palace" hotel back on Seventh March Nineteen hundred and seventy.

It was quite damp and chilly walking along by the river, it was also at times trying hard to rain. I'm pleased to say luck was certainly with us, I felt a lot better when we arrived back at the hospital. I also felt somewhat weary as the streets were incredibly quiet away from the traffic and on hearing someone walking behind you, and then on turning round seeing no-one sent a shiver down my spine and the hairs on my arm stand up "Brrrrrrr." Your mind can play silly devils and when you are told that street muggings are up in the area it made me wish I had something to defend myself with.

Well with the weekend approaching quickly and still no word from the paediatricians who we're looking after Amanda; we were again becoming impatient; there was no slacking on testing's carried out on Amanda. In fact, the determination and desire shown by all the medical clinicians proved completely and utterly the opposite. Every day they were carrying out something in fact the photograph below Amanda is having some test done.

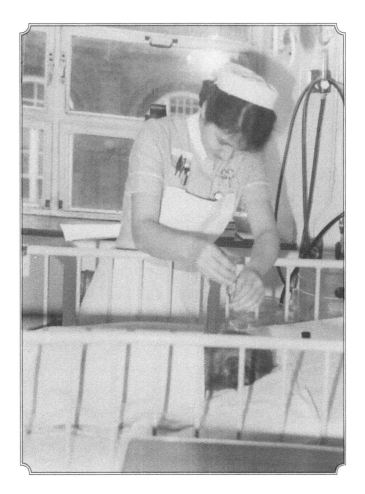

As if there was nothing else that can cause us a problem in our lives since getting here, we now find ourselves being called into the hospital administrators office. It reminded me greatly of a time when I was a child being sent to the headmasters' office at school, by a really pissed off teacher who had taken a real dislike to my schoolboy attitude. "Oh yes"! I had my moments believe me, but then I did attend a Boarding School "The Royal Alexander and Albert" but that is enough about me that is another story for another day.

We knocked on the office door, "enter!" as we opened the door, we were confronted by a well-built woman in her fifties wearing a grey coloured jacket which appeared to be slightly on the tight side either she had put on extra weight or the jacket needed some urgent adjustment as the buttons were taking a lot of strain preventing the jacket from dare, I say it springing open. Her shoulder length hair was neatly pinned back using a very colourful hair clip, so It kept away from falling across her eyes, sat on one of those chairs that sat us down in her office and proceeded to explain the hospitals Parking policy in great length, clearly from her draconian attitude parking on site was a criminal offence, there was no leeway excuse to the parking policy.

We were told politely to move the car as soon as possible if it was not removed it would be clamp it and we would have to pay a hefty fine to get it back. I was told there was a parking area about three miles away from the hospital where we can put the car, as this was the first time, I had driven to London could I be given understandable directions at which point I was handed a street map of the area. We asked how would be able to return to the hospital, fortunately, it was on the bus route that stops just around the corner from the hospital. She didn't know what number (fantastic) but we the position we were in we had no choice, I asked if we could go to the ward quickly and inform the ward staff where we we're going and then get some money to take with us.

Amanda had at this point had still not returned to the ward so after collecting some money we drove out of the hospital; I tell you I was scared stiff; the instructions were as you might guess nowhere as clear as when she told us. I knew from the trip down people who drive their cars on the streets of London are clearly Kamikaze drivers, but my eyes were opened very quickly to London night driving. Like during the day your attention to other road users isparamount but at night your concentration must be double as night driving in a place one is not used to is difficult to say the least, you just cannot make any mistakes and if you did car horns would show the drivers anger blowing with almost every move one took.

Black taxis cabs cutting everyone up, and what is more all cabs had either dented back doors or missing car parts, we drove for over an hour could we find this so-called car park, not in a monkey's eyeball. I was not going to waste any further petrol or come to that open me up to possibly having an accident trying to find this stupid old parking area, I felt sick to my stomach my right foot was shaking badly due to changing from accelerator and breaks. The fear I had trying to find my way back to the hospital was not a job I relish not in the dark anyway, there were blinding red lights directly in front and white lightsappearing to mix with the red.

Making the journey an even worse experience as I have never driven night times through a city before, I was so relieved when a set of traffic lights turned red a Black taxicab pulled up next to us. I got Yvonne to wind the window down. "Excuse me!" "I'm slightly lost can you tell me where Great Ormond Street hospital is?" yes "mate!" was his reply "London" well that was the final straw I totally lost it, and the air was thick with looking back I can now see the funny side but at the time; when he said it my stress levels hit the roof.

I had been driving round London filled with nothing but a crazy kamikaze driver, drivers trying to get to whatever destination and at any cost how did they manage to pass their driving test? Not one driver cared about any other road user around them cutting everyone up this is just mental, I just had to get off this road before I am involved in an accident. As luck would have it an opportunity arose one hundred yards further on as I approached yet another set of traffic lights, Yvonne pointed out a sign ahead directing drivers to Gt. Ormond Street hospital. Suddenly all that stress I felt drained from my body, my feet stopped shaking I still had no idea where I was as we turned the corner, the hospital could have been miles down the road thankfully it was not.

In fact, as I rounded the corner there on our left all lit up like a Christmas tree appeared the hospital, unfortunately I was unable to turn into the street as it was one way. Driving a little further I came upon a car dealers' shop, pulling over I parked up an entered the dealership. Explaining to the gentleman the problem I had encountered he allowed me to park my car on his forecourt, I had to leave a note on the car dashboard telling whoever questioned why I was there and where I could be contacted. Although not happy with having to leave it there I was assured it would be safe as the police constantly patrol the area, The gentleman who later proved to be the owner informing me he was aware of the problem, on many occasions he allows drivers to park temporarily overnight on his forecourt overnight. It must have been my lucky day, or there again it might have been the terrified look on my face as well as a shaky voice that made him take pity and allowed me to stay there for two days instead of overnight. This human gesture of kindness however welcome at the time was in my opinion unusual allowing me to park for a couple of days. What I did not know at the time was less than five yards or so past his shop was a large underground car park, this proved be invaluable to me so, the next day I collected the car and drove it to the underground multi-Car Park.

As I drove down a slight incline, I was stopped by a large red and white wooden barrier a young man in his late twenties early thirties appeared from literally out of nowhere asking if he could help me. I asked if I could park my car only to be told that this was a private parking facility for resident only, clearly, I began to panic as I did not relish the thought of yet again battling the London Kamikaze drivers looking for somewhere safe to put my car. I explained to the Parking attendant the desperate reasons for my position and said I just need to put the car somewhere safe; I do not wish to drive it as I am at the GOSH (Great Ormond Street Hospital) with a seriously ill child.

I will pay anything just to leave it there until I must return home, to cut a long story short he kindly allowed me to park, but it would be down two levels and not to worry about the cost, he would work something out. He also stressed that this would have been between us and no one else. As I walk away, I felt more relaxed in myself and I thank "God" there are still people in this world who have compassion.

I walked onto the ward to find no Amanda and no Yvonne, not knowing what has happened I asked the staff nurse who informed me that Amanda has gone for an EEG and ECG as she has been continually having seriously strong Grand-mal seizures. Looking over her diary the hospital struggled to accept my figures so I recounted every seizure we managed to identify; in many ways I wish I had not decided to count them as to date the tally has now exceeded 1,201,261 remember these are only the seizures; we have personally witnessed.

Amanda returned to the ward about two hours later, the doctors had heavily sedated her, and it was in some way quite a relief to see her no longer flaying her arms crying and calling out as she pulled her legs toward her bottom. Her head pushed back and turning to the right causing her body to twist made even worse as one arm fists clenched extended and the other drawn into her chest. All this traumatic body action would be combined with violent jerks that shook the hospital cots, it had to be seen to be believed an awesome sight.

The paediatrician looking after Amanda came on to the ward, he had some results on Amanda's problem emphasising these were not conclusive at this stage. he confirmed Amanda was really an extremely sick little girl the delay referring her to GOSH, clearly affected any chances of preventing these variety of some if not all of Amanda's condition. So please can you tell me why it has taken so long, Amanda should have been referred at the age of three weeks when this was first diagnosed.

That statement alone made my blood boil, I have been saying that since day one but did doctor. Back listen NO! did he heck it was allegedly in my opinion that his refusal to refer Amanda for independent Investigations because he wanted the Gold Star for Solving this mystery. I felt so mortified I had to Struggle to prevent my thumping the hell out of either a wall or a door, had doctor. Back walked on the ward at that point who knows what I would have done certainly he would not have walked out the same way I can assure you.

Anyway, I had to listen to the other results which I can confirm the findings of doctor. Dutter were close to the diagnosis found by GOSH doctors. Because the diagnosis and cause were still a complete mystery we were asked if we would allow Amanda to be part of an international conference being held in the hospitals lecture hall, it was explained that Doctors, as well as senior paediatric Consultant's from around the world were attending, he would like Amanda to be a Case Study. It was quite a scarry decision to agree too but if it would help to give us a greater understanding of her illness then "Yes," I must admit it felt like we had just willingly agreed to medical practitioners using her as a lab rat but we could not now refuse after agreeing.

Amanda was having a nasty day with major seizure today more than eight hundred and fifteen you could hear her screaming two wards away; it was clearly affecting some of the nurses and they called for a paediatrician to decide how they should move forward. Doctor. Robert Williams arrived a tall man, "oh yes" he must have been at least six foot four tall and of a medium build. His hair was very thin and wispy, gold rim thin framed glasses sat like a tiara on the top of his head. Rolled-up and poking out of the pocket of his immaculately pressed white open coat which flapped violently behind him suggested he had only now come on duty and apologised for taking so long.

Clearly one could see that he was quite upset with the position Amanda was in and agreed that some drastic action had to be done, looking at Yvonne and me he told us that he was going to give Amanda a large dose of Valium and he hoped she would calm down enough to relax and sleep. Dr Williams took Yvonne and me into the parent's room and explained that he has had too seriously sedate Amanda to allow her to rest as much as was possible, they are struggling to control the seizures and in a small young child this may not have a successful outcome. "So, Dr Williams are you telling us that you might never be able to stop them and that Amanda might not survive"? Tears ran down our faces and I found it hard to breathe, I was shaking at the thought that Amanda might die. "I'm sorry Mr and Mrs Cherry" "Amanda is an extremely sick child how her little body has managed to cope all these months with these extremely large grand-mal seizures have us all concerned, at some point the strain may become too much for her.

The problem we are really struggling with is that Amanda's condition has no known medical diagnosis you would think there would be some reference in medical books that could throw light on the issue; but there are none we can find. Therefore, we are calling it the "Amanda Cherry Syndrome." While speaking to us we noticed from his quivering voice he too like the many others who treated Amanda found it difficult not to un-professionally become attached and like his colleagues were unable to withhold his emotions as the tears ran down his face.

Wednesday morning at Ten Thirty Amanda and yourselves have agreed to attend a conference, we might get some valuable pointers on her condition and how we might proceed with her treatment. Yvonne and I were struggling with the fact we might lose Amanda, what did we do wrong? Should we have demanded Amanda be taken to Gt. Ormond Street months ago. If she does die it would be my fault and I could not live with that "No Never" Yvonne and I have never prayed so hard in our lives, and spent a great deal of time in the hospital chapel a beautiful peaceful ornate building as you can see from the photograph below.

Chapter Eleven

THE DAY OF THE CONFERENCE

Yvonne and I arrived on the ward to find that Amanda was coming out of her sedation, everyone seemed more relaxed than usual. It appears that they wanted to see if her seizures were in some way under control, both in strength and quantity we could not believe our eyes as our prayers had been answered on all count. She was still twitching but not continually and were spaced well apart, she was being fed with milk through a nasal gastric tube placed down her nose I shuddered just thinking of it.

Doctors were on doing their rounds and Amanda was in the last cot so it would be a little while before they get to her, Yvonne and I told the nursing staff that we would get some breakfast and hopefully they would have seen her by then fingers crossed. "Full English breakfast I think"! naturally I would have a bowl of rice Cornflakes first, Yvonne said she was not hungry and had Cornflakes, followed by a slice of toast, baked beans fried egg and a cup of strong tea. Naturally, me being me, I was still hungry so went up for a second helping and believe it or not I spied a terrine full of freshly made French fries, so I piled a load over my full English I even covered them in tomato ketchup "Yum! Yum!

After a mug of sweet Coffee, we returned to the ward where the Drs had done their rounds and the nurses had found Amanda a beautiful frilly pink with white trim dress, I had to ask how they managed to put her arms through the sleaves with all those tubs and whatnots attached to her body. Smiling like a Cheshire cat as they answered "by" "Magic!" and like a fool I almost believed it too. There was an air of anticipation as today we will be answering Questions at medical conference arranged by Gt. Ormond Street Paediatricians with expertise in the field of medicine from around the world, what questions would they ask? Do they examine Amanda physically? Or would they give the same outcome as Dr Williams?

We did not have to wait long as a phone call came into the ward asking that we be taken with Amanda to the conference room, it was not too far from Amanda's ward in fact it was one floor up and right opposite the lift which naturally we took for safety reasons carrying Amanda. I am pleased to say we were not on our own as staff nurse Wendy Piper accompanied us and remained with us so she said to help us with any awkward questions should they ask.

As we entered the room, we saw a large rectangle table sitting round the table were twelve men and three women nearly everyone were clearly over fifty years of age, all suited and booted except the ladies they were dressed in skirts and dresses. A youngish man oh he must have been I don't know about late thirties mid-forties with a handlebar shaped moustache asked us to take a seat, he was well-spoken and pronounce his vowels with a posh voice he also had a large bowtie bright red as I recall and wobbled up and down with every word.

They each in turn had questions for us and it I'm pleased to say was nowhere as daunting as I was expecting, we were asked if there were problems with Amanda's birth? "No was our reply" but we did mention to them that Yvonne's immunity to rubella was rather on the low side and the doctor looking after Yvonne decided to give a booster rubella vaccine, Yvonne asked the question of whether it would be harmful to Amanda as she intended to breast feed her. He convincingly informed her that it would not and gave it to her anyway, she was such a beautiful baby not a wrinkle on her face or her body.

We informed them that Amanda also had jaundice for about a week and her GP was considering having her admitted to hospital but it was not necessary as her complexion was normal on his next visit. We were asked if Amanda was feeding well, we mentioned that she would not settle down as four ounces of milk failed to satisfy her, so on advice from her GP we added a baby teething rusk with her feeds which proved to be a job well done.

Apart from those questions all our answers were "No," or we did not see any issues, we were not even asked if we had any questions for them and nor did they even physically examine Amanda. As far as I was concerned this exercise was just a complete waste of time, given the time we spent with them, I suppose they had read Amanda's medical reports and all we did was confirm what was recorded. Amanda was asleep as we headed back to the ward, I'm not surprised Yvonne and I expected to have been hammered with questions but no it's a meeting where professional doctors kept looking at each other round a table mumbling a few words only directing the odd question now and then at us "quite mentally deflating in my opinion."

Yvonne and I were in the parent's room having a cup of tea when Doctor Williams walked in on us, "Just to bring you up to date with the outcome of the Conference" he said. "I would love to report that Amanda's situation was well known, unfortunately" … "here we go again!" … "Amanda is proving to be a challenging case with a baffling number of overarching conditions, such as Liver dysfunction, severe brain damage, Blind, severe cerebral palsy, and a pronounced twisting of her spine not seen in a patient of her size and age all at the same time."

The outcome of their discussions was as follows… Amanda was suffering with Gran-Mal- Seizures this diagnosis we already knew, why they felt we needed confirmation was really beyond belief; they were just confirming the same Results we were already aware of.

We were so angry that I accused Doctor Williams of repeating all the tests carried out by all the hospitals before naturally he denied All my allegations, he explained the hospital has been working and continues to work desperately hard trying to find the reason for Amanda's severe illness. In fact, today they are going search for possible allergies such as food colourings, Shampoo, Soap, washing powder, dairy Milk, Aerosols and yes, they will be testing for any reaction to the rusk biscuits we have been giving her.

We were rather puzzled on how these tests were carried out, he explained "we put small patches on her arm with a minute drop of whatever solution that needs testing and after a few hours we check the results. Well, that was a new step for us or at least if it has been carried out in the past, we have either forgotten or were never told. Amanda is off all her drips only has a nasal gastric-tube and a canula in the back of her right hand, as you can see, she is looking quite ill today nurse Angela Feldmann is cuddling Amanda she is certainly, one of the many nurses who have fallen in love with her?

It is now twenty-two minutes past eight on a Friday night, having spent well over nine hours at Amanda's bedside feeding and giving drinks through her NG tube (Nasal gastric tube), It proved quite problematic at times for us as we had to keep moving out of the way. Which was unavoidable as the ward had a total of thirteen cots all with a seriously ill child was occupying if there were a real problem [Emergency Yvonne and I would leave the ward and only return when the issue had been resolved].

We both quickly realised that this happened quite regularly throughout the week, this gave me a chance to update Amanda's life story and allow us the opportunity to try and relax [impossible!] Doctor

William's has informed us that he has a result back from the allergy testing several days ago, it showed a possible reaction to cow's milk and have now put Amanda on a special powder milk called "SMA" and hopefully this will stop any reaction in a couple of days. My stay at the hospital is about to end and I must make my way home to Lowestoft, I had no idea how quickly time flies and that three week is quite short.

I really did not want to go but the medical certificate I have runs out on Monday and I will have to renew it also, the free car Parking will end on Sunday. I am rather concerned that I may have caused a slight problem, throughout the three weeks at the hospital, I have been telling parents that they might be able to park up for free if they kind of stretch the truth a little…. well, a lot really. Just explain that your child has been admitted to GOSH and you are not allowed to park your car on their car parks, and if challenged say one of the hospitals consultants suggested you contact the parking attendant to see if he would allow you to park up in the residents parking area well it certainly worked for me.

Chapter Twelve

THE LONELY JOURNEY HOME

Well, the dreaded day arrived; I was starting to panic how I was going to drive home through London, I had no idea of the route I would have to take or whether I could find a garage open so, I could fill up with petrol. My stomach was churning as the nearer the time to leave got the more it seemed to get worse, I did manage to get some breakfast down me but at the same time I was fighting to keep from throwing it back up.

If anything was going to settle my nerves, it was in the knowledge that the trip ahead of me was on a Sunday and I was told the traffic would be a lot less, the added concern of course was trying to find the A12 back to Lowestoft. There was no point hanging out the fact I had to leave so I said my goodbyes to Yvonne and Amanda and made my way to the car park, it was just past two thirty and it was beginning to cloud over and I was hoping it would not rain. The car park attendant was not in a good mood and informed me that lots of people have asked if they can park their cars as they were told by a Doctor at the Hospital it would be possible, he asked if I had told them naturally, I said "no" …. Well, I certainly we're not going to tell him that it was me and more pleased that they said a doctor had suggested it.

It was clearly obvious from both his body language and the way he was looking around avoiding personal eye contact with me that he really wanted me gone, so when I asked him about the cost, he immediately told me nothing if his boss got hold of the fact, he had allowed people to park without charging it would cost him his job, "I said thank you" "that's OK" "but if you do come back don't ever think about bringing your car here"!

I had no intention returning to London by car not in a month of Sundays, I only did it this time because I had no other Choice if I wanted to be near Amanda and Yvonne. Finding the car was quite an ordeal as I had not returned to it since I parked it there three weeks ago, eventually in a concealed corner alongside a large white pillar I found it only to discover would you believe two other cars identical to mine were parked close by "how weird is that… eh?"

As I climbed into the car it felt cold and damp not surprising as it had not gone anywhere for three weeks, I was also worried about it starting as the engine had not been turned in that time. My concerns were laid to rest as she kicked over first time, although my petrol gage was reading half full so I would need to fill up as soon as possible. I was certainly not sure what the traffic was like, but there was a "Shell" about a mile or so away. It finally took me three and a quarter hour to get home just in time as Yvonne's mum just dishing up tea, boy it was so good to see Anne-Marie as she ran down the path and gave me a massive hug. It was not long before Questions were being thrown at me from all sides, I had to stop them and gave them a report on what had gone on while in London, I had arranged with Yvonne to stay by the telephone at Seven thirty and I would call her. Mum was on the phone well over the hour and Anne – Marie had to talk to her mum and asking the same questions of her much the same as she had asked me, I wondered if she either wanted confirmation on what I had told everyone or was I just making things up.

Come Nine o'clock the pressure of the journey home had taken its toll and I was ready to go to bed, I decided to get home have a bath and then bed. Tomorrow was going to be quite busy as I had to make an appointment for the doctor, I needed to renew my medical certificate and to make sure the DHS (job centre) had a copy and to sign on again. That was going to take up most or all the morning, I also promised Anne Marie I would take her shopping in town. Anne Marie has lost out on being with mum and me and she has put up with a lot, it was time for me to spoil her a lot. After the shopping trip which she enjoyed immensely I took her to a fish and chip restaurant on the sea front to round off the trip, boy I forgot just how big her appetite was not only did she finish her food but also enjoyed finishing off mine as well.

Being home again was fantastic but my mind was continually kept in overdrive wondering what was happening in Great Ormond Street, Yvonne was alone and I unable to give her any physical or mental support if needed. I telephone Yvonne saying I intended to return next week all being well, I would not be driving down and would come instead by train. Anne Marie wanted to come with me as she needed to see her sister, the problem was that of getting her home again as I wanted to stay there. There a way around the problem and that was bringing Yvonne's mum and Sister Joan down, it was their suggestion and it would allow them to see Amanda as well.

I also felt it would be an opportunity for Yvonne to have a break and go home for a week or so, reluctantly Yvonne said "no!" at first but explaining it would allow her to have a break and build up her strength for the next round of Amanda's journey. Yvonne reluctantly agreed So, mum and I would book some rail tickets for next Friday, early booking generally cost a lot less than on the day. When I told Anne-Marie she was over the moon with excitement when I say excitement, I mean screaming and running around like a headless chicken, the noise was quite deafening to be fair.

Chapter Thirteen

RETURN TO GREAT ORMOND STREET

The next few days seemed to slow down to a snail pace, and I thought Friday would never get here. When Friday came it meant we had to catch the straight through train from Lowestoft to London's Liverpool Street Station at the early time of six-fifty in the morning and arrive in London about eleven fifteen am, What we did not think about was Friday was a school day and finding a spare seat was not going to be easy. We also never thought just how long the train would be, with eleven carriages and a dirty green coloured Diesel locomotive the whole train was longer than even the platform.

I was quite surprised that by purchasing our tickets early we had reserved seats, I found out more by luck than judgement as I our names appeared on cards that had been placed in cardholders sown onto the top of the seats. We were placed in the eighth carriage of the train almost at the back of the train, before leaving the station to begin the three-hour fifty-minute journey our carriage had well over twenty noisy school children and that was unbelievable.

As we arrived at each station on our way to Ipswich more and more and more school children swamped the carriages till it became so cramped the children we're finding it difficult not to bump into each other, those passengers who had seats were constantly being hit in the face or shoulders by their satchel's. The guard struggled desperately to move down the carriage to clip or sell tickets, and no one dare struggle to get out their seats unless they were getting off.

Eventually we arrived in Ipswich, to everyone's relief the carriage became almost empty as the school children exited and only about thirteen people including ourselves remained on board. After about a five minute wait the train moved out of Ipswich and began to make its way to London, eventually arriving at Liverpool Street station about mid - day and as usual with the train services across the country, we were late not by much four minutes to be precise and would lay that at the feet of the maintenance department that delt with line maintenance /signalling problems.

We had no issues with getting transport from the station to the Hospital with Black Taxis by the bucket load in fact I have never seen so many in one place, as one took a fare another moved up and just like a roller coaster another took its place. We reached the hospital in about seventeen minutes, the driver said we do not need to worry about ordering a taxi now but to ring when we need it. As we walked onto the ward Yvonne was having a cup of tea, Amanda was still sedated and was being tube fed. I think it shocked the family to see Amanda lying there with several intravenous lines attached; I explained each line had the purpose of either administering a drug to control seizures. In Amanda's case urgent regular daily line changes were required, so rather than un-necessarily re-moving the IV's only to re-sight another every time it was better and less traumatic just to replace the tubing.

The Ward Sister advised us to get some food from the staff canteen as Amanda was booked for an ECG, and it would be at least a couple of hours, "Good Idea" I said the meals are particularly good and you have quite a choice on the Menu, the girls stuck to a salad, and I had favourite steak and kidney pie with chips peas and gravy. On our return to the ward Amanda was crying and she needed to be comforted with a cuddle, Anne-Marie was in like a shot and who was going to stop her I could see the rest of the family were also keen to hold her.

Quickly time caught up on us and it was soon time to consider leaving for home, I was going to remain at the hospital and Yvonne was going home for a week to get some "R & R" she was looking somewhat tiered and I'm sure the break would do her good. Amanda was sound asleep by Seven o'clock tonight and it allowed me to have an evening meal in the restaurant followed by a short stroll to the River Themes and back, it was quite chilly and naturally like a man I did not take a coat or jacket that's not going to happen again especially if I walk along the river.

Despite the fact it was chilly I enjoyed the break from the noise generated by the trollies squeaking wheels, it gave me the chance to gather my thoughts of the time spent while in "Great Ormond Street." I was even told that yesterday a young Arab boy had been admitted for a serious life-threatening operation and that the family had taken up a whole floor, his father brought all his household with him "I wonder just how much that cost?" It was about nine thirty and it started spitting with rain when I got back to the hospital ward, Amanda was quite restless and had just been given a sedative to help her toward a more comfortable nights rest. I retired to my room and phoned Yvonne to see if they had a good journey home, apparently, they nearly missed the train due to traffic and an accident on the way to the station but made it by a hairs whisker.

Anne-Marie was worn out and was asleep in bed. I said if there were any change in Amanda's condition I would phone and let her know. After tea I made my way back to the ward, Amanda had been moved to a side ward why? I asked just for a change of scenery I was told. Deep down I thought it a little funny that now they had decided to move her, I found out later it was due to the fact the BBC TV were doing a documentary and they might include Amanda as a subject to film and meant it would be better if she were in a cubical rather than having a TV Crew on the ward.

It never happened of course but the chance was it might, I was quite please about that as Amanda and I had not had our hair cut. After the BBC crew had left, I was asked if I minded giving Amanda her tea, Silly question butnevertheless, they gave me a two hundred and fifty mills jug of thickish milk. The milk was called "SMA," and I had to give it to Amanda through her Nasal Gastric Tube, after feeding her I flush the tube through with clear water and prepared her for the night rounds.

Having disappeared to make a coffee and have a fag telephoned home to update the family of the events of the day, I returned to find an exceptionally large black nurse frantically giving Amanda C.P.R instantly I turned on my heals and rushed out of the ward my head was everywhere and physically shaking as I made my way to the parents waiting room. I simply panicked, I had only left Amanda for a brief time. I walk in on nurses rushing round, alarm bells ringing" all I knew was if I stayed, I would not be of any help either to the medical staff or to Amanda I would certainly be obstructing, shaking like a leaf I had to remove myself immediately from the room.

The human brain is a wonderful thing I had lost all sense of time, sound understanding everything had shut down. The feeling of fear being torn up inside, I have never since Amanda was born walked in on the sight of a nurse physically working to save Amanda's life. My head was in overdrive was this what Dr Back predicted would happen to Amanda, was this the end was she going to Die? "No" stop thinking like that it is just a little blip she'll be fine!

At least that was what I wanted to believe; God would not let us down I trust in him.

Somehow while everything was going on around me, I had managed to fill the room with smoke. My eyes were watering and stinging I did not realise that I smoked two packets of Benson & Hedges Super king size fags and the mug of coffee I made I had not touched; it had gone cold and had that disgusting scum on the top. I had no idea how long I paced around the waiting room; I became aware of someone calling out my name "Mr. Cherry!" Malcolm; "Mr Cherry!" I felt an arm around my shoulder and soft voices directing me to sit down. Are you ok Malcolm? We saw you leave the ward in a hurry and you seemed to be worried, Amanda is fine she just gave us a scare; it is her way of letting us know she was still here. I was so stressed out that just hearing those words I broke down; they took me to see her myself and showed me that she was fine. I said thank you to the nurse who I minutes later found out her name was "Asha Kamali" from Nigeria, after I apologised for my actions, she told me there was no need to apologise. I have learnt a lot tonight including the fact Asha was employed as bank nurse, which explains the reason for not having an ID badge with her name showing. We spoke for over an hour, she told me she was born on the 27th of July1947 of Nigerian parents. Her father was a doctor, and her mother was a housewife, they emigrated to Britain in 1958 to work as a paediatrician on a paediatric ward in London. Asha did say what hospital to be honest I can't remember but it was not Great Ormond Street that I know, her mother worked as a clippie on London transport before she died in 1979 from a heart attack.

Asha's dad returned to Nigeria, and she has not spoken to him since, but the family do stay connected and say he is not a well man, losing his wife and mum had affected him badly. Sadly, that was the last time I saw Asha; I did ask around but was told as a bank nurse she may have been banking at another hospital in London. Yvonne returned on Saturday, and I filled her in on the excitement Amanda had given us during her week away, also the fact I found it difficult to adjust to the fact that Dr's have stressed this could well happen again, and that we should prepare ourselves for that very real possibility. Not something a parent wanted to have pushed down their throats at every turn of the screws, nevertheless at least they were being honest with us.

Chapter Fourteen

AMANDA'S PLACED IN AN INDUCED COMA

The time is now seven thirty am, Yvonne and I were about to leave for breakfast in the hospital canteen when the phone rang it made us jump out of our skins. It was Carol Samson the ward Sister she called to say Amanda had, had a bad night, her seizures were again, extraordinarily strong and lasting several minutes at a time. So, it was decided to put her into an enforced Coma. I am sure this decision was upsetting for the nursing staff as they have become overly attached to her and it sounded as if she was crying, "We're on our way!"

Arriving on the ward staff nurse Rosemary Black met us again well-spoken and very fiery Ginger colour hair so brilliant it almost appeared red to look at. At the foot of Amanda's Cot was a large looking box, clipped within was an exceptionally large syringe filled with a milky looking solution this was being pushed through a clear tube into a canular placed in the back of Amanda's left hand bandaged heavily and splinted securely.

Amanda was laying on her right side and believe it or not seemed to be snoring or at least it sounded like it, she was also attached to another drip sighted in the back of her right hand it too was bandaged. It really makes one want to cry so I can understand the feelings shown by her nursing team. Rosemary explained the pump was a temporary measure and it was in a final attempt to try and bring Amanda's seizures to some conclusion, eventually Amanda will become so deeply comatose all brain activity will become relaxed. She will remain in status for approximately a week then slowly the medication will be reduced, the idea being that hopefully, any seizures will abate or be greatly reduced both in number and strength. Yvonne and I spent many hours talking to Amanda and reading stories, I recall someone saying people who were in a coma can hear you talking whether that is true or not I have no idea and I have no proof they can't.

It was kind of strange to see her just lying there, your eyes drawn to her chest watching as it rose and fell the only visual evidence, she is still alive. So far to date it is estimated Amanda has had in total some 1,237,177 gran-mal seizures, Drs are baffled on how her little body has survived. I have been keeping a daily diary and struggled with the number of seizures too, not only that I have not been including the twitching or petti-mall's maybe I should consider including them if I should do it, I am certain it will make life as we know it more distressing.

Amanda has now been sedated for a total of eight days and things seem to be on the up, there has been an occasional twitch now and then but, overall, nothing to concern the medical clinicians. Doctors so we have been told are due to do their ward rounds this morning if they are happy with the ward Sister's report, they could decide on reducing the medication and slowly begin bringing Amanda out of this induced coma. They will then know if it has been a success or sadly, a complete and utter failure, if there is a GOD in Heaven, please let it be good news. It will take at least five full days to bring her back, and this cannot be hurried.

Yvonne and I decided that we would go down to the canteen and grab a bite to eat, then take a walk to Covent Garden's then onto Nelsons Column and make our way back to the hospital, hopefully by then the doctors will have completed their rounds and made a favourable decision on the next stage of Amanda's lifting out of sedation. The doctors had been round and the decision to bring Amanda out of her deep sedation had been made and would begin tonight, they insisted it not be done quickly but over the next six to seven days as a precaution and that it would mean watching and monitoring her very, veryclosely.

The job of watching and monitoring Amanda was difficult as we literally took the doctors and instructions to heart and I mean to hart monitoring everything, it was not an easy thing as the fear of Amanda coming round and once more continuing to have seizures as strong or stronger than before. Nursing staff strongly insisted we both take a break for an hour or so, relax and chill out, nothing is going to change for at least a day or two.

Day five has arrived and there is a great deal of change in Amanda's persona she is beginning to react to stimulus and clearly appears more supple in her arms and legs, before she would remain quite stiff and ridged now, she is almost like a rag doll floppy pliable but to be fair she is still sedated. The best thing is she seems to be seizure free up to now we pray it will remain so indefinitely but we are not there just yet, even the nursing staff appear to be more relaxed beside her and this must mean something would you not agree? It's now day seven and the good news is Amanda is out of the sedation completely, "thank you Lord!" she appears to have improved in skin colour and more importantly not a single seizure as we know it has been noticed. Another good thing is she appears also more responsive to noise and people talking to her, Amanda jumped almost out of her cot when the medicine trolly lid slammed closed. Now we are watching Amanda closely just in case the seizures return, not sure if we are now experiencing another symptom on worry or am I really hoping she does start convulsing.

"No!" Malcolm please; I must not increase the overall mental strain and pressure on our lives, these types of action must clearly be struck from mine and Yvonne thoughts: I'm beginning to become paranoid where I should now be just thankful that Amanda seems to at long last reached a turning point and things can only get better; now every day free of seizures is fantastic blessing for both Amanda and us. A young doctor by the name of Sandra Stanford approached us, when I say young, she could have only been in her early twenties or early thirties. around her neck hung a bright red stethoscope and sticking out of the pocket of her white coat was a black one, naturally

I asked, "why two stethoscopes"? only to be told this was left by a colleague so she would return it when she next sees him. "We would like to try and get Amanda to try some solid food tomorrow and would we like to feed her" "she asked" there was no way we were going to refuse, so now we have something to look forward to and we can hardly wait. The day started violently as the clouds were black the rain was falling heavily high wind and thunder and lightning which lit up the sky, at least we did not have to walk through it as there was a connecting underground tunnel to the hospital from the residential family quarters. The disappointing issue was that according to the weather forecast it seems it is in for the day, so Yvonne and I will be able to help throughout the ward as and when the nursing staff require help or assistance. Maybe I can pretend to be a doctor that should be fun.

It was not long after arriving on the ward that staff nurse Jennings asked if we could look after Amanda as they were short on nursing staff, she said they have had to call for some bank nurses to step in. As Amanda was still hooked up to monitors, we had to give her a bed bath, which was fun we put more water on the sheets and blanket than on Amanda. After the bed bath was feeding time, they thought that rather feeding Amanda by NG tube it would be nice to try her out on some solids, this certainly was going to be a challenge. Since her arrival at Great Ormand Street Amanda has been either on a saline drip or NG tube.

The hospital dieticians have drawn up a menu they'd like to start with today:

AMANDA CHERRY (6mths)
Creamed Mash Potato with Steamed Fish

It was pointed out that the mash was made with powdered milk not dairy milk or cream. The fish was steamed; **Haddock,** I think? To follow was a small bowl of **Raspberry Jelly** bitterly sharp taste. Amanda did not go much on the Creamed Potato's and fish; well, it did not smell very appetising if I say it Myself and it tasted just as bad. As for the jelly now, that was clearly a vastly different kettle of fish Amanda could not get enough of it, and it went down as if really there was not a tomorrow. Drs were jubilant over the fact Amanda tolerated the solids and she kept it down liquid food was still being given via the NG tube but only as a backup should Amanda require it. (Night feeds were still maintained and drinks via NG tube every two hours). It was considerably exciting to see this remarkable change in Amanda, have we reached a new critical moment of change in Amanda's life? Have the medical experts at long last managed to discover a miracle drug. Questions? Questions? Questions?

Our excitement has become somewhat overwhelming, Amanda seems to be more alert and is responding both to voices and physical touch. As for seizures we have not witnessed one, but the most exciting change is in her eating habit nothing much seems to affect her at this stage. The menu's change daily, we tend to be consulted on ideas of what to try mostly the dietitians agree with the suggestions, but very rarely do they say no as it might be pushing the boat out a little too far at this stage.

Doctor. Wilson arrived at about eight thirty and did not seem to be overjoyed to say the least, "Mr & Mrs Cherry!" "Amanda may have another problem in that it appears her Kidneys are not really functioning as they should." "Over the last few days, we have been monitoring urine levels and regrettably they have been exceptionally low, this has been backed up with several other test carried out including blood tests." Tomorrow, I have ordered a kidney scan just to see if we can discover possible reasons," What else is the good lord going to throw at Amanda has he not thrown enough at her.

At the time Yvonne and I failed to understand the serious complexity of what Dr Wilson was eluding too; he was obviously experienced enough to see we were clearly naïve in our approach to Amanda's plight should the tests come back positive. We were not so flippant in our attitude by the time he finished explaining the Possible outcome, the sombre knowledge that it may be life threatening if damage to both or even.one of her kidney's would prove disastrous. The concerns felt by Dr. Wilson became evermore poignant as he had also arranged kidney scans for both Yvonne and I as well, our scans had been arranged for ten thirty tomorrow morning. We were both very frightened as they we're thinking of compatibility for donor matching.

This has now changed the playing field, what if neither of us is compatible matches then what? The thought of this started to jumble our brains, the more we dwelled on the negative the more frightened we became and the stress we already had become intensified to physically wanting to vomit. We both felt petrified, our stomachs churning, fearful of the scans but more importantly the anxiety of the results. Amanda has not been to good either today crying for most of the day to, something we don't know what was going on the crying was the same as when she seems to be in pain. She was thrashing her legs and arms about pulling out the NG tube and the IV drip they had to reinstate; I cannot recall the last time Amanda was this bad they were going to sedate her with Paraldehyde.

I really hate this injection with all my heart body and soul as it must be delivered intramuscularly with a glass syringe as it is an oil base medication with a large needle. Amanda's poor little legs were heavily bruised by constantly injecting her, her bottom was red raw from the rectal Valium and had to be covered in cream to give relief from angry soars on her bum even that has an oil base to it. All we need now is for Amanda to start having seizures again, and we will then be right back to square one. We were also told Amanda was being slowly weaned off the steroids she was. having as the doctors think they are not working, I thought she had been off them for some time obviously not.

The Paraldehyde did not take long to take affect and Amanda had settled down and fast asleep, I may not like them using the drug, but it can be a fast action miracle. worker. The Strong smell of the Paraldehyde emanating from the Cubical was so heavy the whole hospital ward wreaked of it; it was so strong we were forced to open all the windows to allow fresh air to circulate if not everyone would be knocked out. Yvonne and I decided that we needed some food, what

I did not know because of the actions of today that our spending money was running low and would have to find a bank tomorrow. Clearly living in London is not as cheap as living in Lowestoft. Anyway, we were about to go sightseeing as another examination was planned for Amanda today, Amanda will undergo a neurological test to confirm that she is blind or if she is seriously sight impaired. It would be approximately three hours in length as they would be doing bloods and EEG tests again, they certainly were not going to leave a single stone unturned but then they're again investigations and findings have from day one been nothing but thorough.

The sun was shining, and it felt quite warm the smell of exhaust fumes was at times overwhelming and less so if you happened to be walking by the Thames Embankment, we made our way to Nelson's column and marvelled on the size of the enormous black lions, the hight of the column and even more impressed by the number of pigeons in one area. Seeing Piccadilly Circus in all its glory with all those neon advertising billboards which flashed continually both day and night lighting up Cupid on his pedestal; "fantastic."

Almost three hours had past and before we knew it, we found ourselves back on the ward, Amanda had returned and as usual had been sedated and remained asleep. The results hopefully will be with the medical practitioners later today, seeing as it was lunchtime. Yvonne and I made our way to the canteen. Steak pie chips peas were on the menu and is one of my favourite meals. Amanda has come round from the sedation by the time we returned from the canteen, unfortunately, she is rather grumpy, but I think it might be she is thirsty or more likely hungry so the nurse in charge of Amanda ordered a bowl of potato fish pie.

I'm sure this must be a standard meal anyway Amanda seems to enjoy it, raspberry jelly for pudding finally for a drink was warm milky tea this was given by NG tube. We had just finished feeding Amanda and prepared her for bed, when we were approached by two young looking doctors, Doctor. Robert Christian he must have been 7 feet tall, and a young female doctor great deal shorter about 5 foot 4 inches tall. Quite Small in stature and from India, I am ashamed that I remain unable to pronounce her name. She was wearing a beautiful multi-coloured. Saree Orange and pastel blue almost the same as Doctor Dutter back in Great Yarmouth Hospital, which also wrapped round her Slim-sized body also her midriff was bare and proudly revealed a stunning deep blue piercing in her belly button.

Doctor Christian told us that he had the results back and sadly they confirmed the findings of their investigations, "not what we were wanting to hear,nevertheless, we had to accept the findings and continue to struggle with the outcome. They are still seriously puzzled regarding the reasons why Amanda is like this, even reiterating the world-renowned clinicians, they have seen children showing one maybe two different symptoms but never all the symptoms Amanda has presented. They are so baffled that they have recorded the results as ***"THE AMANDA CHERRY SYNDROME."*** So, after all thebullish shouting tempers and "YES" threatening behaviours toward many Clinicians we have got no further in finding a Course**, "I'm so, so, sorry Amanda."** Our hearts are broken, the wind has at this moment been knocked clean out of our sails, we will not be giving up; I say this to all who know us as a family it is not; nor will it ever be in our character just to give up the fight.

Yvonne and I now must take all the hospitals tests result and findings try to understand them and start a new battle, a battle which will have many upsetting and tearful outcomes but a fight, nevertheless.

Chapter Fifteen

TRANSFER BACK TO GT. YARMOUTH

Arrangements are in progress as we speak to return to Gt. Yarmouth Hospital, it has been an eye opener for us to see what goes on in the world's most renowned Children's Hospital for Sick Children. We have seen some wonderful sights both happy and sad, children with life threatening issues which both Yvonne and I had the privilege of under supervision and trust help nurses on Amanda's ward (feeding mainly or encouraging children to eat).

With the arrangements to transfer Amanda agreed, they have asked that we see them in the consultant's office something we were seriously concerned about. (it's the fear of not knowing). "FEAR! Is something Yvonne and I have had to live with for the last ten months, every day we wake worrying what we would find when seeing Amanda. The first question to emanate from us was "How has she been through the night?" The responses normally are particularly good, thought the truth is she has been fitting and agitated, Sedation seems to calm her but is not the ideal solution for Amanda.

How do we know she had been sedated? we could smell it on the ward. (Paraldehyde) (Rectal Valium) being the main sedatives used both tend to burn when given rectally, not only that but if the Paraldehyde is administered intramuscularly after time hard lumps appear on her legs. Eventually these lumps do disperse but the damage to muscular tissue would be irreversible and painful bruising remains for several weeks.

Our appointment to see the consultant was for two o'clock, today and we will be able to find out what is going on. Yvonne and I spent the whole morning with Amanda although her seizures today are petit – mal, we know each seizure no matter what size will continue to slowly and irreversibly damage brain cells and inevitably effect the heart muscles. We understand the doctor we are to see is Doctor Robert Belton, unfortunately he was called to an emergency and running late. It was almost three twenty when we were able to meet with doctor Belton, he was very apologetic, and he asked us if we would like a tea or coffee "Please."

He began to bring us up to date on the procedures and test Amanda has been having since her transfer from Gt. Yarmouth, for a couple of days the Clinician needed to monitor Amanda and to build up a picture on Amanda's medical needs. It was obvious there was an urgent need to try and control her grand-mal seizures, a job proven various Hospitals Amanda has been in. It was clear the drugs she was prescribed had no effect and investigations of the many anti-convulsant medications on the market would take some time to work, investigations Amanda has been subject too are as follows all under sedation: Brain Scans. Complete Body Scans. Uncountable Blood tests Numerous Changes in anti-convulsant Medications, many unsuitable for Amanda Condition.

Scans that were taken to keep a check on her little Heart (heart was closely monitored). Bone density (carried out with regular Blood test). Liver and Kidney Scans. They even checked the functionality of her spline. Believe it or not checks were also carried out on Yvonne and me, liver, kidney, blood. Including a full body scans checks to check the checks of the checks of procedures carried out in case they had missed something, anything. Nothing arose with any procedure undertaken so that was disappointing for them as it was for us, all the test done came back negative.

With all exhaustive tests complete it was decided by consultants to return us to Gt. Yarmouth Hospital on Friday mid-morning. Disappointment could be seen on our faces not to mention the deep sadness and hurt within our hearts, we we're not satisfied with the decision and begged the clinicians to keep on trying there must be more they can do to find the reasons. As sad as it is Amanda's needs must be considered she has been through hell and back enough is enough and to continue to put her through further procedure's would be unjust and criminal just to continue getting the same results.

Friday Morning was upon us, and we would be traveling back to Gt. Yarmouth at about 11 am, the ambulance arrived at 9.30 am Amanda was being prepared to be transported. We have never seen so much equipment for one person, there were at least three boxes and two bags placed in the back and excluding our 2 cases luggage which together doubled as a makeshift table. As for Amanda she was still attached to Drips and a pump infusion of I think Valium but they would not tell us, and Amanda was placed into what I would call a premature baby pod.

She had oxygen silver foil and blankets around her, the thing is it is not that cold so will she not get too hot?

Anyway, while Amanda was placed in the Ambulance, we said our goodbyes and that was certainly, an incredibly sad and emotional moment, we had naturally become rather attached to all the staff on the ward and to be saying goodbye would prove over the coming years difficult. We were assigned a staff nurse to accompany us in the Ambulance, she was in her early 40's very pretty and slightly on the plump side her name is Angela Wilson who presented as a very competent nurse and certainly meticulous in her methods.

It took almost 45 minutes to get out of London, Amanda had been lightly sedated or at least relaxed sleep. Once clear of London the ambulance crew made up for time lost, we are heading for Newmarket and a need to refuel. Obviously, I was miss- informed on the capacity of these Ambulances Petrol tank and thought it would take us all the way to Yarmouth.

The journey to Newmarket was not too bad as the traffic was quite light, we refilled with petrol and after a 15-minute break for food we hit the road again. Amanda has become a little restless and is keeping Angela rather busy, it might be she is hungry Angela gave her some warm milk she had in a thermos flask we're not required to do anything but watch. All this was done through the NG tube, it really did not calm her down and for Angela this was quite concerning. Amanda's blood pressure began to drop, and her breathing became erratic, we were some 30 to 40 minutes from Yarmouth. Angela wasted no time lent forward tapped the driver shoulder and signalled for him to put his foot down. The response was instantaneous on went the blues and two's or in laymen terms blue flashing lights and sirens.

Yvonne and I were in a real state we knew that a problem had arisen but not how serious the situation with Amanda was, Amanda in a calm and professional way gave us both an assuring glance and explained as best she could what was happening and that the crew had radioed ahead to the Bascule Bridge in Lowestoft and requested that they do not lift the bridge till we have crossed. Nothing is ever easy with Amanda and would prove to remain so for many, many, years to come.

Chapter Sixteen

WE BELIEVE IN MIRACLES

We arrived back to find that the old Yarmouth hospital had closed and anew one called the **"James Paget"** had opened on the Lowestoft Road in Gorleston, while in London there were changes made Yvonne and I had not heard or seen and really surprised us. There was a fresh strong clinical smell as you walked in through the Casualty department, fresh paint and new colours washed the walls it even had automatic opening doors into the A & E department.

After a lengthy dash through the hospital corridors and lift ride we finally arrived on the Children's Ward right at the far end of the hospital, we were placed in a cubicle so small it was as if we were still in the Ambulance. The cubical even struggled to contain a hospital cot, the life support equipment for Amanda had to remain outside the cubicle. Amanda along with all her special equipment had to be physically taken off the trolly by hand and placed onto the hospital cot, our cases, and bags medication etc were delivered by hospital porters and squashed in the corner of the room. It literally was not what we expected to find in a brand-new hospital.

With nowhere to sit or get some rest there was another problem we were made to endure, for over forty-five minutes we were made to wait before the duty doctor arrived to examine Amanda. This upset the nurse from London's Gt. Ormond Street as the Ambulance had to return, calls were put out but it seemed to fall on deaf ears. Eventually the senior ward nurse arrived and the handing over responsibility to the hospital took place, Angela was at long last able to return home we thanked her and wished her a safe journey back to London.

We regrettably were not so lucky as once again we had to bring doctor Back up to speed with what Amanda's treatment had been, as if he could not have read up on her medical notes. With booking in done and Amanda due a feed Yvonne and I left for home, she was still in a status and medication was now due. Amanda has now been in and out of hospital and nothing has been found to suggest the reason for Amanda's problem, so we really are no further forward with a definitive prognosis. The horrifying fact is that Amanda has several times now been close to death, if it were not for the medical staff both in Gt. Ormond Street and in Yarmouth Amanda may not now be here. Amanda has just reached the age of Nine Months of age and the battle still goes on, Yvonne and I will continue to fight tooth and nail to insure she gets the medical help required and I shall continually be breathing down the neck of doctor Back.

As the weekend rapidly approaches Amanda has been struggling with feeding, increased seizures, breathing problems keeping anything down was neigh on impossible. Everyone's concern was how to control the issues she has presented the medical staff with, clearly at this time it has become easier to sedate and enable rest. Is it this down to the cocktail of anti-convulsant drugs? "God it could be anything" If only we had answers! The struggle and fight we had to get Amanda to Gt. Ormond Street even though the eventual outcome was not what we wanted, gave us a feeling of security a comfort blanket if you like.

Now we have returned I feel that we have gone a full circle only to be back where we stated all those weeks ago, the nursing staff are in my opinion so dedicated no amount of anger I have is directed at them. My anger is directed at one consultant, "Doctor Back." These are the rock, the foundation stone, of the medical world and clearly are above reproach, doctor Back is the hospitals Senior consultant a man who has an extremely high egotistical attitude. Anyone who I have spoken to has not a good word to say about him, including dare I say many of his professional Colleagues.

He is in my opinion, and it is my opinion, a man allegedly who needed to add yet another trophy to his medical career "the I enjoy playing God" what I say goes they pull the strings. As long continues as to get his mega bucks whatever that is; he appears to complete control of the hospitals administration, so now once again, my battle with doctor Back will resume the worrying thing is I know I am not going to win even with the support of other hospital staff? "Sorry!" I have again allowed my emotions to get the better of me, I have allowed myself to verbally vent all my anger and frustration though this media but it is clearly in some close friend's opinions taking my personal feelings unnecessarily over the top. They may be right as I clearly do not feel any better for it, "what the hell can I do" "I detest the man with every breathe and bone in my entire body!"

We had been back in Suffolk now three days, Amanda really has not been well She is back on the main ward with two other young children. One a little girl who has had a hip procedure carried out her legs covered in plaster of Paris, there is a small, short round pole it is used to spreadeagle her legs keeping them apart. she hangs suspended from a cradle anchored by a metal frame attached to the cot. The child is forced to hang upside down and at the same time struggle to play with the toys placed near her, I have been assured that they do allow her to lay on the cot both to eat and to sleep. Still, it clearly is not comfortable no matter how long or short the hanging is, the other child is an asthma sufferer she was rushed onto the ward late last night but seems to be a little better now.

As usual we arrived to find a nurse dressing Amanda, she had just given her a bath and preparing her for our visit. We continue to monitor her hospital notes that are placed at the bottom of the cot, "why do we do it?" well there is the issue that when we ask how she was during the night we tend to be told she has been comfortable. Yvonne and I are not stupid, but we understand the reasoning behind the replies, so reading those notes tell us exactly how she has been in fact we have go quite good at it. Naturally, we have read things that worry us and we have followed through with asking the Paediatrician's to explain a little deeper.

Testing investigations have less since our return, I think they are more into preventing the seizures and improving Amanda's food intake at present. In someway the relaxation is allowing Amanda to rest from the pressures of evasive procedures (sticking in needles being the prime culprit), Amanda has slept for most of the time we were on the children's ward. Walking to the car tonight, it was plain to see someone had been having a wonderful time, every car had a flyer placed under the wiper blades inviting people to attend a local Baptist church laying on of hands.

Some drivers clearly were annoyed screwing them up and just throwing them on the ground, as for me I folded it up and placing it in my coat pocket decided to read it when I got home. Not being a devout religious person, well not since Amanda's illness began made me lose faith, how can this so-called God allow innocent young children to suffer in the way Amanda has? Surely this is not a test to see how we would cope having a child with a serious disability, or did he decide these people would be ideal parents needing a challenge in life?

Did not sleep well last night tossed and turned no idea why, I got up at 5.30 am I went into the kitchen and made myself a coffee and a Branston Pickle sandwich. As I was up, I decided to clear out the fireplace (BAXI BOILER), it creates a large amount of dust and if not cleared out daily like any fossil fuelled fireplace causes inevitable break downs a lot. The last time it broke down we woke to find the bungalow flooded all our carpets in the front room was squelching as we stepped on it including the hallway, luckily, we have floorboard throughout but drastically the channels between the joist were filled and had to be pumped out. That took us over 11 days of continuous pumping, a further 3 months to dry out the wood and treat it with water repellent in a hope it would work. Any way that again is another story for me to possibly tell in the future should I find time.

Arriving at the JP this morning late, is because we had to do some much needed grocery shopping. It hurts us to be away from Amanda even for a short time, I am positive she experiences the same awareness as we are awfully close family group. I spoke to the Ward duty Sister Jane Munro, "Sister while going home last night we found this flyer under the window whippers" showing her the flyer she glanced over it. "I know that Amanda is seriously ill, but I will try anything that might help her," "what is the possibility of taking Amanda out of hospital to attend the churches laying on of hands?" I swear

I heard a very faint sinical chuckle at that request I was surprised at the answer sister Munro gave even though she chuckled at my request, "I will ask the doctors tomorrow but don't hold your breath."

Several days went by without hearing a word, Sister Munro had been on her days off. Naturally, we were oblivious of this and not surprisingly we have not had the luxury of taking breaks since Amanda's illness, she had sent a message though and it was just as expected "NO" they reminded me of the fact that Amanda is still a seriously ill little girl. I was to be fair disappointed and upset but understood the serious nature of my request, hopefully over the next few days or weeks thing may take a turn for the best.

A week went by and there was no sign of improvement in Amanda's condition but there was also no worsening either, we have seen this happen so many times, before creating a false sense of things reaching a turning point before the shock horror the resurgence of seizure's starts up again but more violently. Her seizures have reduced in strength but remain clearly visible and that is of course due to the cocktail of anti-convulsant the doctors have her on, There has been no visible change as expected in Amanda's condition nor was it ever expected if the truth be known, once again in my opinion doctor Back lives in what can only be described as a dream world. His attitude toward Amanda's situation unfortunately remains the same as when she first became his patient, it will always be, "she is my patient!" He alone will decide on how progress will continue medically while she is under his care.

Yet another flyer has ended up on our car, something is screaming in my head and heart does not voice anything like that but increased eagerness to try again to see if we might be able to take Amanda to this Baptist Church service. Once more with a I flyer in my hand I approached the Ward Sister, it was Sister Munro's day off another sister by the name of Rachael Stone was on duty instead. More importantly I was told doctor Back had gone away for a few days, a much younger consultant was standing in for him.

A doctor Stanley Morrison walked on to the ward he must be 30 to 40 years of age and an athletic body to boot at least 5 foot 10, I think he spends a great deal of time working out in a local gym it was just like young nurses in a movie were in a childish way sniggering and whispering behind their hands. He has an unruly mop of curly ginger hair on his head, hair that seemed to have a mind of its own it just would not lay flat and appears windswept. A rather thick ginger beard covered his chin and a deep broad Scottish accent in his voice.

He eventually arrived at Amanda's Cot, after reading Amanda's notes examining her without lifting his eyes said "Sister informs me you would like to take this wee lass to a local healing service tomorrow?" "Yes" I said, and showed him the flyer. He spent a little time reading it, the church was less than 10 minutes from the hospital. "Before I give you an answer, I must do some inquiries and then I'll get back to you" he said. There was no way he was going to allow us to take Amanda out tomorrow, she was hooked up to so many IV drips and pumps drugs you name it Amanda had it. Apart from that he would liaise with doctor Back and we know what his answer is going to be, I wish I had not made an idiot of myself by asking.

We did not see Doctor Morrison again, nor the following day we arrived early on the ward and prepared us for disappointment in allowing us to take Amanda out and attend the Church service. It was about 4.30pm the wards staff nurse Betty Carter came to tell us that a lot of thought and worries and concernsaround allowing permission for us to take Amanda tonight, the good news for us is that putting their cards on the table weighing up the pros and cons both for and against the safety of Amanda's must be high on the agenda. It came down to the commitment from us to return her back to the ward in time for her medication and feed, we can take her out. For a moment or two you could have knocked me over with a feather,

Yvonne and I were beside ourselves we were as I said before expecting the answer to be, "Sorry;" but "NO" the illation we were feeling made me want to kiss staff nurse Carter. It was not going to be a simple action to take at six PM Amanda had all the cannulas and drips removed but the NG tube remained, her arms and hands were black and blue where the cannulas and IVs were sighted it really looked as though she had been seriously abused. The feeling of are we about to do the right thing? What if something goes pear shape, we would be held responsible. I was not feeling at ease with myself, my eyes remained transfixed on her praying everything would work out well,

We were quite nervous when we arrived at the church, it was quite difficult to find as it was situated up a side road. The church was made of red brick and pitched slated roof, a large arched frontage with two large wooden doors faced you as you mounted several steps the left-hand door was wide open just inside the entrance door was a narrow table and chair. The table not only draped with a white tablecloth with yellow and red edging. A large bright light hung from the ceiling: a lady met us at the door introduced herself as Mary and took us through to a vast benched seating area.

It was mind blowing white walls at least eighteen feet high drew your eyes to large black wooden beams, each of the beams were anchored to each other with exceptionally large black bolts. Three 7-foot-tall stain glass windows created a prismatic display of colourful light around the room as the low late evening sun shone through, four wide stairs led up to a deep reddish looking stage with a preaching pulpit and choir seats to the left.

At the centre of the stage were four people with guitars, a percussionist, a Violinist, and double bass player, to the left of them an exceptionally large projector screen used to project the words of the hymns for the congregation. As for the congregation there was at least 80 to 90 people there, Yvonne I think I spent most of the service watching arms and hands uplifted it was truly and incredibly mind blowing, she said. After singing a couple of hymns the main reason for being there arrived, the Minister asked if anyone wanted to receive healing would they like to make their way to the stage. Oh, how I wanted to get up and go, Seeing Yvonne and I with Amanda in the stalls he asked us to remain seated he and his prayer group would attend us there, he eventually reached us sat down next to Yvonne and Amanda he asked, "What is the name of this child?" all the while gently stroking her head, "we have brought Amanda out of hospital here as we received one of your flyers. We explained that Amanda is seriously ill and has been in and out of hospital for most of her life, we explained that doctors both hear and at Gt. Ormond Street in London are unable to diagnose the reason for her illness.

"What might that be; If you don't mind me asking?" "She Suffers from Grand-mal seizures, is Blind, has severe Spasticity in her arms and legs, and if that's not enough her body is cursed with a serious spinal curvature which we understand will become worse with age and growth." Finally, so mystified by exactly the cause the medical profession has name it the "Amanda Cherry Syndrome." Clearly the emotion of what was being explained got to both the minister and the congregation who were involved in the laying on of hands and those who were prying I noticed just how much as tears rolled down many faces.

The minister and his colleagues remained by our side praying and blessing not just Amanda but also

Yvonne and I together, naturally there was never enough time to remain too long we had to get Amanda back to the hospital as promised for her medication. Returning on time meant that if we wanted to take her out again, we could be trusted to get her back on time, as it happened, we felt seriously guilty we had certainly overstepped the mark this time as anything could have gone terribly wrong placing Amanda in danger. The fact it did not, proved that we were lucky and got away with it, I feel we had to try anything but not again.

Amanda had most of the drips and tube replace immediately on her return and had a feed put down her NG tube, sadly she was quite restless when Yvonne and I left at ten o'clock it was quite dark, and we were hungry, so as usual we called in at the Chippy who luckily finished at eleven PM. The events of the day enabled Yvonne and I to discuss between us the various aspects of today's events that happened, I know we had no problems, but what if?

Amanda was quite peaceful today we managed to get onto the ward at Seven thirty still suffering the effects of last night, we did not get to bed till two AM this morning discussing our actions now we will have to wait for a slagging off from doctor Back. That is going to be overly exciting as a few days have gone by without some form of altercation between us, Consultant's ward rounds were typically, late, and hopefully will happen later this afternoon but that is anyone's guess. Staff nurse Carter oversaw the ward today, it seems that Sister Munro had food poisoning and will be absent for a couple of weeks we wish her a speedy recovery.

Amanda was strangely quiet with the odd petti-mal seizure, although not too worrying any fit is not good as it can continue to damage Amanda's health. Pleasing to know the cocktail of anti-convulsant medication is helping to suppress the larger ones, Yvonne and I felt we might go home early and relax as much as we could. As we walked out of the hospital it was slinging it down with rain, so hard it was close to Biblical proportions, the road and footpath were literally swimming in water. It almost appeared like fog and stung as it hit your face and hands, I had parked the car someway away from the entrance and naturally, both of us were drenched through to the skin, our sopping wet clothes squelched loudly as we sat in the car. This was no fun the clothing nearest to our skins were freezing as we lent back in the seats, we just wanted to get home to change and get dry. As we started to warm up windscreens fogged up, trying to demist them proved difficult.

Putting the cars heaters seemed to make things worse, opening the windows slightly for a brief time made the visibility of the front windscreen a little better but only for a brief time. The heavy rain hitting the car was frightening as the wipers could not cope, an unpleasant experience as many drivers who have unfortunately had the same problem will vouch. Next time we will bring an exceptionally large umbrella, we will eventually learn from our mistakes.

Amanda was being Amanda today, they tried to change her NG tube and she was determined to disrupt it. She kept on sneezing and coughing it out, crying closing her throat off so forcing it to come out of her mouth. I have never seen that before but the nurse said it is a common occurrence with patients of Amanda's age, what they tend to do is go away and let them rest and return later to try inserting it again. Their decision to not struggle to replace it was a concern to us if not to them as now Amanda would have to be given a bottle, getting her to suck on the teat proved nye on impossible she just spat the teat out. We tried to enlarge the hole in the teat that had no affect apart from causing her to choke cough and throw up, patience is certainly a virtue but this moment in time was something we had not managed to learn.

After an hour struggling the nursing staff returned to try again, determined to put the NG tube into her tummy via the nose. "Why do I say determined?" well this time there was two of them, "If it fails this time" they said "Amanda has an IV canula with which fluid can be given" at this very moment although sited in the back of her bandaged and splinted left hand it was not in use. It just goes to show how observant we are and would normally ask why her hand had been splinted and what for, I thought it might be for administering urgent medicationhow wrong can one be?

We went home at Ten-fifteen and left the staff to sort Amanda out and would return early tomorrow, Amanda was still in an angry mood and to be honest it was starting to stress us both watching it all unfold. What would Yvonne and I find on our return would be anyone's guess? The stress sadly took an upsetting hold on us and we had an unpleasant drive home, we shed a few tears this was as far as we recall shown us another side of Amanda the side the nurses during their shift would witness daily. For our mental state we were being told that Amanda has mostly been fantastic, now we know this was not the case and would in my opinion rightly or wrongly explain her constant sedation.

While in Gt. Ormond Street I personally walked in on a scary moment as Amanda was receiving CPR; I was eventually told that this has been a common problem. "Why have we never been told?" "What else have hospitals been constantly holding from us?" Now my blood is boiling this has got to stop as Amanda's parents we should be kept in the loop, it all about trust openness and confidence that the nursing staff have not only Amanda's back but ours too. Questions will be asked I assure you especially when consultants do their next ward rounds, withholding critical information on patients' treatment surely is illegal especially regarding a minor of her age.

Yvonne and I were once more feeling reluctant to leave her, God knows what might happen what we have uncovered today has really damaged out trust in what we are being told by so called medical professionals. "Yvonne and I at this moment let down hurt and unable as I said earlier to trust anyone!" As you might expect there was a feeling of trepidation as we walked onto the ward, there seemed to be a change on the ward we have not seen for an exceptionally long time. We walked onto Amanda's ward and met the most exciting sight it was a miracle we could not believe what we were seeing, the side of Amanda's cot was put down two young nurses had Amanda propped up with a large puffy V shaped pillow and they were feeding her with a jar of cherry treat, all the canula drips NG tube had been removed and she had shown no sign of seizures.

It was explained to us that after we had left last night Amanda began coughing and gagging, she had pulled her NG tube almost out of her nose they had managed to replace it earlier in the evening but after half an hour she tried removing it. Amanda had completely change doctors were called and even they are unable to give an explanation, never in their entire medical experience have they ever seen a change like this in any of their patients. I have been asked many, many times if I believe in miracles now, I can say without hesitation "YES!" thank you "Lord Jesus!"

Chapter Seventeen

DREAMS CAN COME TRUE

Amanda spent another two weeks in Hospital after this miraculous change in her illness, the so-called medical geniuses may never have an answer to what may have caused Amanda's conditions. I am but now I'm totally and utterly convinced that a higher authority has stepped in, we have prayed, begged and blead buckets of tears so, so much for God to step in I think he must have been listening and heard us praying. It just meant we had to have faith in the Lord physically prove our full commitment to Amanda and bringing her too the Lord to be blessed, our faith has been restored in him thank you.

Doctors were satisfied that Amanda had improved mysteriously over the last four days they are discharging her tomorrow, "hurray Amanda is coming home" our minds are going wild with excitement we can hardly take it all in. Nursing staff are truly, emotionally excited they have travelled every step of this long painful journey. We gave Amanda a jar of Hinze vegetable broth lunch it did obviously tasted better than it smelt, anyway Amanda ate every spoonful. We will call into the supermarket before going to the hospital and buy some jars of Hinze baby food.

It was close on mid-day when we arrived on the ward, the Nursing staff had put A beautiful pink laced dress the sleaves were edged with lace and what looked like a white laced bib, around her waist was a loosely tied pink belt her hair had been brushed to one side top off with a beautiful hair clip pink socks and shoes. Staff Nurse Carter said "Amanda has had a good night; we gave her a lovely bath and she has had her breakfast Wheat a Bix half a bowl and ate the lot." All we must do is wait for her drugs and discharge letter, which can take hours to turn up it is a well-known issue that hospital pharmacies tend to be laid back and slow as can be testified by many patients.

Finally, Amanda has her discharge letter, but her drugs did not arrive on the ward until three-thirty PM, which was due only to the fact one of the nurses had to go and collect them. Well; all we are eventually on our way home, we never thought we were escaping the clutches of doctor Back and his iron fists. Amanda has managed to leave something behind, baffled minds on how the change in Amanda's condition but taking away from doctor Back the opportunity to say I've diagnosed reasons why Amanda's was how she was. (TUFF!).

Amanda slept well all night and was still asleep at nine o'clock this morning, Malcolm was running a bath while I stripped her down. This was going to become a daily routine from now on, as Amanda was soaked through there was also, the need to change the sheets on her cot. Amanda was very stiff and tense, our bathroom was quite small, and one could hardly kneel, but we learnt to make do. Another problem was the bathroom was at the end of the extension and quite cold to boot. We wrapped Amanda up in a soft blanket and took her into the Lounge, Malcolm had prepared a warm fire. The living room was long and narrow about eighteen feet by ten feet including the furniture, there was a three-seater couch deep red in colour from the kitchen door and a high back kitchen chair one of those that had a seat that lifted out.

A door that leads to the corridor aloud extra light into the room, finally there was an alcove I think that is the name about eighteen inches deep. I know it was a devil of a job trying to wallpaper, it was about a good inch out of square and we needed to use a plumbline to get the wallpaper straight. Jotting out into the living room was the fire, a Baxi boiler jet black in colour with a glass door. Next to that was an airing cupboard this house at the bottom the central heating pump, pipes, and some cleaning equipment.

A largish picture window allowed the main light into the room, unfortunately our neighbour's house was about six feet away shaded us from a piercing sunlight. As they too had a window opposite ours, we were able to see though into their living room. So, to allow us some privacy we both had thick net curtains, underneath the window was our folding table which when we pulled up one leaf took up half the living room. Next, we have a self-made DIY work bench well that's what I call it, there was ample room underneath to store odds and ends such a boxes and cleaning equipment.

It was very sturdy and had our TV and a various other item on top, it was also strong enough for Malcolm to climb on. Naturally, I have not mentioned wall decorations such as Photograph's or picture of which there were many. The front doorbell rang I opened the door to see two young ladies, they introduced themselves can I remember not on your life. All I remember was the fact it was the district nurse and a colleague, well what do expect my mind was on other things at the time for heaven's sake anyway I invited them in. They explained that they are visiting us to find out if everything was OK and to check on Amanda as she has just been discharged from the James Paget Hospital, while the district nurse examined Amanda her colleague began asking Questions. "How has she been since coming home? was she sleeping and eating Well? and how were we coping in ourselves? There were certain questions we could not get our heads round as they in my opinion did not seem relevant at the time and still don't, I told the young lady the best thing that has occurred is now we are home we are a fully functional family once more. It might in the minds of some; unaware of our Families history; struggle with that statement but we are a a family of three, Anne-Marie has been clearly suffering while her little sisterhas been in hospital. She has been through no fault of her own greatly missing out on the bonding with her sibling, she has been living with her nanny and Granddad only seeing us occasionally.

Now all that is behind us Anne-Marie has stepped up to the wicket and gets involved in everything, she helps to measure out Amanda's feeds bathing and dressing cuddling her sister as many times as she can. We might as well sit back and let her carry on, she is fantastic, and Yvonne and I are so, so proud of her. With the completion of medical checks, the district Nurse was satisfied, she would return next week and if we have any problems, we were to call her anytime on her personal phone number. I asked them both before they left what their names were, I felt embarrassingly stupid.

Anyway, the district nurse would you believe it, was called Anne-marie and her colleague who was a Social Worker was called Jenny. she was rather helpful, looking around the house she seemed to be concerned with some of the rooms "Front room, Bathroom, Bedroom" and thought we had a chance to qualify under local medical legislation or something like that to possibly help with urgent home improvement for Amanda's health lifestyle. "Please leave it with me" she said "I will speak to some officers in the office see what can be done and get back to you,"

Two months have now passed, and Amanda has been fantastic, no sign of seizures but her feeding has still some way to go. We take her out and make her life as natural as possible, but it's not; not really, we are always ladened down with essential bags Amanda's change of clothes, her medication, clean nappies, feeds all having to be placed on top of her trolly it almost appears as a mobile tank. "Hey-Ho!" we could be looking at Hospital visits or worse, we have met and made friends with much the same problems as us looking after children with all sorts of disabilities. Until that happens to you; one has no idea how many families are presented with the same type of problems, such as heads turning, starring eyes, whispering that a big one to cope with talking about person with a handicap in front of them while clearly in front of them and looking down on them.

While out on a day trip to Hunstanton such a problem arose two middle aged ladies: they must have been in their late fifties; early sixties; whispering and pointing fingers, toward one group member. It got a bit too much and before we knew it, she launched at them with language I've only heard from mouth of a fisherwoman. Sadly, it is our society of today and the ignorance of mankind "How do I know that" I heard someone say?" "Easy" I said "I have spent a great deal of my childhood around fishing towns but more recently fish markets including Lowestoft" it is not acceptable I know but that is the way society is and will regrettably be so for years to come I suspect.

Yvonne and I have lost so much time with Amanda that we shall for many months try to catch up, we are determined to give Amanda as much as a normal family life that we are allowed. Trips out experiencing the good things in life, knowing that she will never see what life is like she will have another streamline sensors built for example Hearing; smelling; touch sensory. Happy emotions, and even amental ability sensory enabling her to know she is greatly loved by us her parents and the many friends we have made so far in her life.

Our weekly attendance at Gorleston's Baptist Church has greatly change Amanda and continues to do so, People have commented that there is also a noticeable change in Yvonne and me. We seem to be more relaxed appearance. our body language is notably changed we appear to be less guarded and or tense not seen in a long time. Amanda has been seizure free for over 5 months isn't it fantastic, she is eating drinking and appears to be in her own way enjoying life. This is all "GODS" doing long may it continue; we realise that while like this it is only time before Amanda's improvement will end and we return to status quo. We pray that this is an exceedingly long way off, each day she remains like this gives her time to gain strength and reduces any further severe damage.

Chapter Eighteen

WIND OF
CHANGE

L ife has a habit of turning turtle and throwing spanners in the works, and yes you guessed it we were not excluded from the spanners. Amanda has been so good over the last 5months but that was about to dramatically crash, at eight fifteen we were awakened by a piercing scream; Amanda was having a seizure so strong it caused her to almost stop breathing (holding her breath and coursing her face to appear red bluish in colour). She was twisting her whole body her left arm was so ridged we dare not attempt trying to move it to her side, her legs were pulled to her chest, her eyes rolled back showing the whites of her eyeballs. Amanda's whole body was in spasm and jerking violently, her screaming was replaced with a grunting puffing sound spittle was oozing from her mouth which she was sucking in and out causing it to froth like frog spawn it is the only way I can explain it.

Yvonne and I were in tears, panic has set in Yvonne called Doctor Kelly and it Seemed to take ages for the surgery to pick up the phone. The receptionist said "Doctor Kelly is not in today could we bring Amanda to the surgery?" Yvonne angrily shouted down the telephone "Amanda nor we are in a state to be goinganywhere... she is having a major seizure and we are running round like a headless chicken" "Ok I'm sorry stay calm!" she said that's a laugh, what a statement to make "I will get Doctor Markham to call urgently."

Amanda's seizure lasted about 28 minutes, long enough to calm ourselves a little but making us watch her very closely just like a hawk Doctor Markham eventually made an appearance at 6.30 pm. He was a quite tall slim man well dressed and clean shaven, by then Amanda has had 3 more grand-mal seizures not as this morning but nevertheless, it seems we havereached a wind of change. After a full check over Doctor Markham was not happy with her condition, she was still having small seizures and although we were unable to physically see them, he detected them through his eye glass thing used to check a patients pupil dilation her eyes were flickering from side to side quite rapidly.

It did not take long for him to decide that Amanda needed to be in hospital and here we go again, both Yvonne and I were really upset as you can well imagine Amanda has been fantastic, but we allowed our minds to think she would never be ill again ("How pathetic and stupid can we be"). The ambulance arrived within minutes and Amanda and was rushed into Lowestoft Hospital, I followed in my car finding somewhere to park was easy there was a space on the hospital car park I think I took a consultants parking area did I care, not a bit.

The doctors wasted no time in administering Valium and Amanda was out of it again, a call was made to the duty paediatric consultant a Mr. Reginald Stewart middle aged grey haired full grey beard and a monocle, "yes you heard me right a gold rimmed and chain Monocle." How does he manage to hold it in place? He was wearing a light stripped grey suit, a red carnation in his button hole light brown laced up shoes and a strong chalone. Finally, he sounded like he had possibly attended Eaton College with a prim and proper voice.

Amanda had been in Lowestoft hospital for less the four days, there was tubes and IV lines everywhere they had even placed one on the top of her left foot. It was held in place with a bandage as were all of IV sights, it was heart breaking to be witness to what can only be described as a legal form of experimental lab testing on a human being. Yvonne and I could not help to publicly cry, as she was being constantly monitored every ten minutes.

Every day was made difficult but knew we had to be strong, Yvonne and I have had to remain strong for the family's sake. Again Anne-marie found herself being looked after by her Nanny and Granddad, for an eight-year-old Anne-marie has been fantastic I've said it many times before and will always say; "for her age she has been a real trooper!" Apart from counting Amanda's Seizure even while sedated we needed to take some time for ourselves, we were so emotionally drained you could see it on our faces and our actions. It did not take much to push us over the top, Malcolm had already flown at one of the nurses over a silly remark passed between two ward staff members. He knew as soon as he opened his mouth that he was in the wrong, unfortunately he was close enough to hear the remark. Any way we did not feel like eating, instead M Malcolm made a cup of tea and coffee while I had a bath and then took to our bed.

We were startled by the telephone ringing, Malcolm slept on the left side of the of the bed next to the phone, you can imagine deep sleep and the closeness of the phone caused us both to jump from the bed. It must have rung for about a minute while we regained our senses, it was the duty ward Sister in the Lowestoft Hospital's Children's Ward. Looking at the alarm clock next to the phone it read three fifteen in the morning. "Mr Cherry. Sister Pat Smith at the children's ward Lowestoft Hospital," "Amanda has taken a serious turn for the worse could you please get here as soon as you can?"

Fear and Panic; Yvonne began sobbing "What the bloody Hell has happened?" Our thoughts were non existing, "what were we going to find when we get to the hospital?" It did not help trying to understand what was going on as we both were clearly not fully awake due to the hour of the night, we were met at the entrance to the ward only to be escorted to the visiting room. A doctor Martin asked us to take a seat, "Mr and Mrs Cherry!" he said "I'm sorry Amanda had a massive Seizure just after 8.45pm, the panic button was pushed and we struggled for 5 hours trying to stop the seizure, (283 in total). Her vital signs were lost 3 times and we had to resuscitate." He said "Amanda is fine at the moment but we are not sure how long for?"

Our lives have just been giving a crushing blow, emotions were running high I was physically shaking from top to bottom. This was a nightmare this was not happening; we were hearing voices but muffled as if behind closed doors. I felt a comforting arm around me, Yvonne was being comforted by one of the ward nurses who also was very emotional. Doctor Martin said. "I see from her medical forms she has not been christened or baptised now might be a good time." I did not answer him my mind was oblivious of my surroundings sounds everything muffled someone grabbed my arm I think, and I was facing the reality of the moment, "sorry!" "I lost it for a moment" I said. My head was clearly a million miles away. "Name of your vicar?" "Oh; yes!" Rev William Hill St. Marks Church Oulton Broad. Was this to be the premature time span for Amanda survival, her tiny little body eventually succumbed it was questionable when she was in Great Ormond Street but managed to bring her back. Had doctor Back's estimated survival prediction of two to eight years been drastically overestimated and now come early, like a large slow turning drum my emotions were all over the place.

My whole body was shaking my legs felt like jelly my whole body in fact was in shock, Rev. Hill arrived he was shocked as he was a friend, he tried to console us both before officiating the Christening Service. We were in floods of tears the process was so relevant and raw to us as we were about to say good-bye to Amanda, naturally I was not going to stand quietly as the time drew nearer. I found myself sitting on a wooden bench under a tree as I looked up the sky was clear not a single cloud the stars twinkling as they do; I shouted out in a loud voice. "God why are you doing this?" "Why now?" "Come on answer me!?" "Again and again, you have punished Amanda, again and again you have tested us why, why, why!?" "If you are going to take her then do it now, if not then get off her Bloody Back."

If anyone has ever been in a position of stress and anger like this will Know it is so physically draining on your body, I found it difficult to breathe for some time as if I had just sprinted for five hundred yards. I took several minutes to regain what little composure I could in the circumstances, I knew it was not going to change the fact I had to face the next stage of Amanda's last moments: moments so precious I was stupidly losing out sitting here on a wooden bench when clearly my place should be at Yvonne and Amanda's side.

I was unaware that time had flown by so quickly, looking at the clock in the main entrance I had been sitting on that bench swearing at God for nearly an hour. Reaching the Children's ward Yvonne caught site of me and came running toward me, she was crying and shouting throwing her arms around me she screamed "where the bloody hell have you been!?" "I've been looking for you for the last thirty minutes. "What's happened?" I asked. Between her crying and erratic breathing I could not understand what she was saying, she dragged me to the small ward where Amanda was and I nearly passed out, there before my eyes Amanda lay propped up with a V shaped pillow minus all her tubes IV's and being fed a jar of "Cherry Treat."

I was told Amanda had become very agitated throwing her arms around and kicking her legs, they thought she was having a major seizure when in fact she literally had decided she would not tolerate her NG tube any further. The consequence of the flaying of legs and arms unintentionally took care of the IV's that must have been painful just in itself, also it is not an enjoyable act to replace any IV sites again. Amanda is playing games with our emotions and mental state, I do not like it at all, but the outcome of this episode has proved to be a good one I must get angry with God and to shout and scream at him more often. "Thank you, Heavenly Father, Thank you!"

Chapter Nineteen

HAPPY FIRST BIRTHDAY AMANDA

As I sat quietly in our living room remembering moments of past few days since Amanda was discharged from Gt. Ormond Street to Lowestoft, I was aware of a change mentally. Amanda has been her usual self-up and down giving Nursing staff the run around (bless her little heart), but for me I have been unable to remove the fear that is destroying me within. The true reality of doctor Back's prognosis way: way back, and yes over her time spent in various hospitals that it became whether we like it or not same prognosis to us by many other medical Paediatricians.

I have been fighting so; so hard to prove the doctors wrong my mental stability has become deeply damaged. Trying as hard as I could to deny what is clearly seen by medical professionals as the only inevitable outcome, in their opinion Amanda will not survive to adult age. Every time I hear those conclusive reports make the hairs on my arms stand up, and testifies completely to my ignorance and total denial of the facts. Moreover, my total and utterly stupidity in not accepting the findings by professionals, Professionals who have trained for many years to get to where they are today has me believing that as a small caveat to that they possibly can and do sometimes get it wrong!

Several days have passed since Amanda pulled out her NG tube and dislodged her IV Drips, she has been clear of seizures and have decided that as she is eating well and drinking orally from a bottle they will be discharging her on Friday three days before her first birthday. Rejoice, rejoice never thought this was going to happen. No more travelling to and frow to hospitals, it will in some way brings a little normality back to our lives hopefully for a long; long time to come. We must not become complacent in our belief this will last indefinitely, we cannot allow ourselves to believe our vigilance can be relaxed now that Amanda seems seizure free for a long time. I am not so naïve as to think that our lives will always be on high alert more so now than ever before. Happy

Birthday to you, Happy Birthday to you, Happy Birthday Dear Amanda happy birthday to you. YES! Amanda is a year old today; she is quite relaxed and appears receptive to loud noises, Yvonne dropped a saucepan lid on the floor and I thought Amanda were going to take off. She jumped and started to cry, but I'm pleased to say she soon calmed down as I picked her up and comforted her. Amanda has had a wonderful day; 18 birthday cards and 9 presents including a couple of teddy bears, she had 9 family members and friends of the family visit the younger family members were rather noisy making Amanda jump a great deal.

We had to take Amanda to Gorleston Hospital for a Clinic appointment as she has now been discharged for Six weeks, having been pushing for the promised home social visitor we were beginning to worry. So, I have learnt that to get anything to happen in this life, one must keep on pushing and pushing till eventually someone decides the only way they can stop the annoyance is to satisfy the questioner and eventually officers give up and authorises the paperwork and surprisingly you guessed it miraculously appears.

We arrived at the outpatient's clinic just after two-thirty, the waiting area was packed with around eighteen patients mainly children aged between three years and twelve. When we booked in at reception, we were told that Doctor Roberts was running late and there would be a substantial delay, we were advised by the receptionist to make our way to the canteen and have a cup of tea or coffee. Two hours later Doctor Roberts arrived only now everyone had become fed up including the children who were running and shouting, even Amanda had become restless and it is not easy to calm her down.

We were very wary as if Amanda becomes too restless it might trigger a seizure and at this moment she has been seizure free, it was 4.30 pm when finally, Amanda's name was called, and I was at my wits end. Frustrated and angry I sadly, took it out on Doctor Roberts, I know it was wrong but someone had to be on the receiving end unfortunately, he was in the wrong place at the wrong time. I did apologise, he did tell me he was aware of my verbal attacks and had witnessed them on the Children's ward. When he said that it was as if a large hole had opened beneath me, but he did see the funny side chuckling as he rose from his swivel chair.

He asked us to place Amanda on the examination couch while he poked and prodded her tummy, he enquired about how she had been over the past Six-weeks? Has she been feeding well? ("YES") any seizures? ("NO"); has she been going to the toilet regularly? ("YES") in fact laughingly I remarked she was doing very well in that department? Working on her arms and legs he did remark she was quite stiff, her limb movements as he pulled her arms up above her head and when stretching them out and physically manipulating her legs caused some discomfort making her cry.

Doctor Roberts said "I would like to see Amanda again in about another 6 weeks as I am not happy with her stiffness, I shall arrange some urgent Physio first." I did say "she becomes very floppy after a hottish bath," regrettably after 30 minutes or so she becomes stiff again. Anyway, we will have to wait for the physio appointment and hope it is not delayed or forgotten about. It was almost 6.30 pm when we left the hospital, which was a worry as we need to collect SMA milk medication nappies and Amanda's favourite Cow and Gate Cherry Treat. Luckily, the Chemist on Westwood Avenue was open till 9 pm.

Life has become less of an issue just now, unfortunately the fear of Amanda returning to status is still a worry. As we monitor her for signs of convolutions it has clearly become a daunting tiering job. Listening out for the slightest sound it has made us become paranoid and jumpy, it is more stressful come night times we have had to purchase a baby alarm and it is fantastic the best thing since sliced bread I would say!

Yvonne and I sat down last night we thought we would count the number of seizures recorded to date, seizure's that we have personally witnessed boy were we in for a frightening shock. We could not believe the figures that we found, the daily diary I kept held a "x" for each seizure. Well over 1 258,728 to date, "Yes, you read it right" remember these are seizures we have personally seen and recorded. We had to count them three times, even we could not believe the number of doctors are totally and utterly stunned by the figures.

Chapter Twenty

VISIT FROM SOCIAL WORKERS

Amanda is not having a good day today; we were up and dressed preparing for the long day ahead. We had to prepare 8 bottles of feed for Amanda and that alone takes up almost half an hour, I had to fill the washing machine as we had about a dozen or so nappies to wash. Terylene nappies have their own odour when being boiled and we have prided ourselves on their whiteness hanging there on the washing line, the downside is that the odour hangs about the whole house for several hours. As I said Amanda is not having a good start to her day it was quite noticeable, crying not interested in eating in fact she was sick three times today.

Fearful that this might be the start of seizures again we called out doctor Nichole's, he arrived 20 minutes later and wasted no time in examining her. Thankfully, it turned out to be a tummy bug and he advised us to keep on fluids for the rest of the day, we kept a remarkably close eye on her just in case things got worse. Amanda slept most of the day and we had no further problems, this lasted for two days by Thursday morning she was quite vocal, if only we could understand what she was saying.

We have arranged a day out with some friends we were all going to meet at the Claremont Pier at 11 am, Lowestoft's beach was quite packed due to warm sunshine and the beauty of the rays shimmering off the water's surface an outstanding sight if I may say before going onto the sandy beach, it was decided that we would buy fish and chips in the pier's restaurant; they cook a fabulous fish and chips meal, we then went and sat down in the community gardens opposite the pier's entrance for a type of picnic. Boy was it hot the sun beat down on us and it felt like an oven with no shade because there were hedges all round blocking any type of breeze there might be from the sea reaching us.

Amanda was covered with a large towel which covered her trolly from the handlebars to the small hood of the pushchair, it was so hot that we decided enough was enough and when we had all finished our fish and chips, we would make our way home. It was not till we got home and saw the damage to the top of our heads and the back of our necks, they were read raw, and Amanda had just a little redness on her forehead and nose. Excellent job we had some cream in the cupboard to tackle the soreness.

After what was a fantastic day, we arrived home to a very warm house so we opened the kitchen door and front room windows to draw through what little breeze there was, Amanda was sound asleep, and it was good to be able to allow her that rest. British weather is clearly and at times dramatically changeable, yesterday ridiculously hot but today quite the opposite heavy rain and very windy. There was no hope in going anywhere today, and anyway Amanda was again, restless reasons why not known.

The doorbell rang and Yvonne answered it, two strange women stood in the porchway dripping wet bless them. They introduced themselves as Jenny Gould Amanda's designated social worker and Dawn Pointon from Waveney District Council apparently, she was one of the councils senior housing officers. They had received a request from the hospital consultants to pay us a visit and they had some fundamental long-term concerns around the needs of Amanda, and the possible adaptations needed to our bungalow. We asked them in a little puzzled as nothing had been mentioned to us, although I do recall being asked if Amanda had been allocated a social worker some time ago but then nothing it kind of got lost somewhere in the back of our minds.

I asked if they would like a cup of tea to warm them up, Jenny Gould began by asking how Amanda was since she has been home "up and down" I said "but we manage, Yvonne's mother only lives around the corner; she has been fantastic and other family members live close by too." Jenny noticed we were still using terylene nappies and said she would investigate acquiring disposable nappies, she would place an order into NHS supply stores also a mattress Sheet for incontinence. It was a start she said and as she grows other equipment would naturally be considered and purchased in the future.

While we were talking to Jenny Gould Yvonne took Dawn Pointon around the bungalow so she could see what changes or adaptations might be required, Yvonne told me later that Dawn Pointon was writing quite a lot in her folder a exceptionally long full report on the bungalow. It was almost two hours they were here and before leaving informed us that they will now return to the office, and discus their findings and agree the way forward at which time they will get back to us. We were not kept waiting exceptionally long, in fact Dawn Pointon telephoned us three weeks to the day to arrange a measuring up. It has appeared The Government have given local councils a large fund enabling them to offer one hundred percent grants for worthy causes, Dawn Pointon had been looking toward funding a major home improvement project for our bungalow. She was calling to arrange another visit and discus not only the outcome of her last visit but to gain our views on the work they intended to do the property.

There really was no time to waste and were wanting to get the ball rolling, both Yvonne and I have become excited and said she could visit on Friday this week as we we're not intending to go anywhere. "What time could we come?" she asked "Ten thirty" I said that will give us time to get Amanda up dressed and fed, it would also leave us the afternoon free should we wish to go somewhere. Bang on ten thirty the doorbell rang Dawn stood in the porch we welcomed her in and with her this time was the council architect, wasting no time the architect began work on the outside of the bungalow.

With tape measure in hand, I followed him round as he measured the small kitchen and bathroom extension at the back. Measuring the back bedroom and hight of the apex roof he seemed to be roughly drawing diagrams and placing figures to them, Dawn

Pointon met us outside and sent sometime talking to the architect and out of ear shot. He was showing her his clipboard and pointing at various parts of the bungalow before walking over to us to explain what they had been discussing, with his job done he said goodbye and he will draw up a draft plan for Dawn to submit to the next meeting of the Planning Committee On Tuesday night next week.

"Ok Mr and Mrs Cherry!" said Dawn Porter "this is what we would like to do," I was expecting Mrs Pointon to say they would not be able to modernise the bungalow to make looking after Amanda's future needs. Instead, completely the opposite and we were both shocked as she rolled out the suggestions from the architect, the kitchen and bathroom extension would be extended by 8 feet into the garden. Our bedroom area would be increased by 12 feet and the largest proposal would be building an upstairs bedroom extension, this would then allow Amanda's future needs and the space necessary for large equipment as and when required.

The one drawback the council architect will give us the planned drawings, but we will have to submit them to be passed we were happy to do that considering we did not have to pay for them to be drawn. "Still sods law and there is always a sods law," comes the dreaded hidden catch. I have always been told by family and friends never ever presume anything is free in life isn't, then just look at what is being offered here. Even I can't look a gift horse in the mouth and then turn it down "eh come on now!"

Three weeks after the Council Officers had been a large thick brown envelope arrived too thick and wide to go through my letter box. Anyway, I had to sign for it. It was rather heavy; and on opening it and removing the contents I found a slip of paper stapled to a large, folded paper document. It turned out to be a set of Plans for extension work to the bungalow, I had almost forgotten about as so much has been going on over the past three weeks. Amanda has not been too good we have called the doctor out twice he thinks it may be down to a bug that is going round and is quite nasty, he has prescribed a dose of anti-biotics and if there is no change bring her to the surgery. The plans would have to take a place on the back burner for the time being, the medication clearly is not working. Amanda has been very wheezy crying and vomiting after her meals at the moment she just can't keep anything down, I have booked an appointment to see doctor Markham as her doctor; Doctor Kelly is not on duty this week.

Dr. Markham did not hesitate in taking urgent action when we walked in to see him, her breathing was very ruckly, and she was sick twice while examining her, she had a very tender abdomen and her breathing he said was quite laboured it clearly needed hospitalisation. "Have you got transport?" he asked "Yes, I answered." He suggested we get her to Lowestoft hospital straight away, he telephoned them to let them know we were on our way. We had to wait for him to write out a letter for the hospital paediatrician explaining the reason he wanted her hospitalised, Amanda was very pale looking, and we were somewhat panicky praying that it was not too serious.

We arrived on the children's ward of Lowestoft Hospital and Amanda was quickly taken to the main ward by a young staff nurse call funnily enough Amanda Thompson, she was a slim young lady with bright sparkling light blue eyes, accentuated by light green eye shadow and light brown straw-coloured hair. Her voice sounded quite angelic it had a calming effect and very much needed at the time, we were offered tea and coffee and was even given chocolate biscuits as well. Paediatrics were informed of our arrival on the ward, unfortunately, there would be a slight delay before a paediatrician would be available "What a surprise!" and would confirm the reason we were offered a tea and coffee when we arrived. Amanda was still crying as if in pain her little body still in the grip of wheezing and breathing issues, the vomiting was still happening but greatly reduced thank God.

Eventually the doctor arrived he read Doctor Markham's letter before taking the next step, he spent a good twenty minutes examining her and witnessed the discomfort and protests exuberating from her mouth as he continued to push and prod her. The more he poked and prodded the more nervous I became, "I'm going to have a fag, Yvonne!" It was hurting me just watching how the doctors and nurses manage to block out their feeling I don't know. I had become so anxious it was almost fifty minutes and three fags later I felt I needed to get back on the ward.

Amanda had stopped crying by the time I returned, the paediatrician had gone but not before placing an IV drip into the back of her right hand. It must have been a problem sighting it as there was some blood on the sheet, also he had wrapped her hand with a bandage and splinted it up to her elbow. On the cupboard next to her cot was a small beaker which looked like it had her medication in, at the bottom of her cot was a long empty packet it belonged to the NG tube which had been inserted up her nose and into her tummy. Clearly, she has been admitted for how long I don't know yet, she has also had some warm milk let's see if she will keep it down, I really do hope and she does so!! It is going to be another quiet night at home, but also a night worrying how Amanda is. We had no intention of being late and wanted to be at the hospital early as possible, and arrived just after seven o'clock the staff were busy handing out the breakfast trays to children. Since leaving the ward yesterday three new children had been admitted, one was an emergency with suspected appendicitis the other two had tonsilitis and were due to have them removed.

We were unable to see Amanda as the doctors were with her when we arrived, strange how one gets the feel of things not being right and you guessed it those feelings proved to be correct. Amanda had so the ward sister informed us as we arrived the Amanda had taken a turn for the worst; doctors had been called at 5 am Amanda Sadly had a massive seizure this morning and it has been a struggle to stop. Taken into the staffroom the staff were clearly upset at what Amanda was going through, their emotions clearly worried us and we became concerned even more especially as the doctors were still working on her when we arrived.

Yvonne and I have come to accept the type of seizures Amanda can present to the world of medicine, all we craved was to be able to be by her side to let her know we were there. Every moment she is like this rips away another large piece of our already bleeding hearts, we remain oblivious of the reasons why she has suffered this set back she has been fantastic these passed months and we thought at long last the seizures have been controlled by the combination of anti-convulsions medication. Obviously, we have been proved to be wrong and we find ourselves back at square one. Amanda was heavily sedated and would remain so for at least the rest of today, the doctor informed us that the seizures she had sustained were possibly brought on by an infection of some sort. Results taken on blood tests hopefully will when they return explain why and then they can be treated with the correct anti-biotics, it was suggested we go home and return in the morning by then they would know more.

We had not been home more than an hour when the doorbell rang, Dawn Pointon along with a work colleague stood in the porchway "Good morning, Mr Cherry" she said, "May we come in?" thank you. After all the niceties had been done, we offered them both a cuppa but was informed "this was not a social visit but thank you!" Dawn had only come to inform us that "regrettably the proposed improvements to the bungalow would not be going ahead," she said "It was unfortunate but after lengthy discussions the planning committee felt it to be too costly and refused permission."

"Well, Yvonne and I are used to disappointments, it would have been fantastic had it only been permitted; but hey!" "What the heck!" Amanda remained hospitalised for just under three weeks, it was clear this would not be the last hospital admittance she would have as she is susceptible to picking up viruses of all sorts. Doctors informed us that Amanda's immunity levels were quite low due to her illness and she would have to be watched closely from now on, if life could not get any more difficult. "So, bring it on, why don't you?"

Chapter Twenty-One

HAPPY THIRD BIRTHDAY AMANDA

L ife has been tough for us as a family, but even more for Amanda as over the past two years she has been in and out of hospital with infections and severe angry seizures. Since her problems began at the age of three weeks her seizures have increased in strength and ferocity, her arms, legs, and torso have during an episode has become like steel. Her body especially her spine appears to be slightly twisted, she has now begun blowing bubbles and grunting including at times grinding her teeth.

Amanda has picked up various bugs which has also caused lengthy hospital admittance, she has become a regular patient in hospital doctor's work and continue struggle every time to control her seizures as well as infection's she has. I have totally lost the plot when it comes down to the medication for her seizures, trying to remember the anti-convulsant is a nightmare. "Epilim, Carbamazepine, Clonazepam and what she is now taking Epanutin," I have not forgotten the cocktail of "Rectal Valium, Paraldehyde intramuscular injections (Nasty!) to name a few.

Amanda's third birthday is tomorrow can hardly wait, sadly she is in hospital because of seizures and has been heavily sedated a dose of Paraldehyde you could smell it in the entrance of the Lowestoft Hospital yes, it's that strong! It must have been bad they try not to administer it unless everything else fails to work, Why the smell is so strong and lingers around for such a long time is because as Amanda breathes it is exhaled from her lungs.

Amanda has today turned Three and it looks as though her seizures have laps to the odd jerk every now and then, doctors appear to be pleased with her response from another drug change. Yvonne and I are tired and feel we need to take some time out to recharge our batteries, for the first time we decided to go and see Amanda after dinner we hated every minute as it seemed to drag endlessly as we continued to clock watched.

I had just finished making some sandwiches for lunch when the doorbell rang, it was a Waveney

Housing officer. "Afternoon Mr Cherry" he said "The reason for my call is to ask if you still wish to have the alterations done to your bungalow?" I had no hesitation in saying "Yes" if I'm honest deep down I have doubts it will ever happen, we have been disappointed in the past. "ok" he said "I'll get back to the office and get things moving." Yvonne and I arrived at the hospital at about one thirty and found the nurses had thrown a little party for Amanda's birthday cake candles card's the full works even down to a stuffed bear in her cot.

A nurse was holding Amanda feeding her with a jar of Cherry treat which she was enjoying, Sister Carol Ross came over to us and said Amanda has been drinking and eating well her boldly functions are good, and doctors are happy to discharge her. Boy was that music to our ears, naturally we require medication to take with us and a discharge letter for her GP. which seemed to take forever to come, nothing happens fast; "like Now!" Eventually Amanda's medication arrived; our eyes nearly popped out of our heads. There were four bottles of anti-convulsant medication (Phenytoin), Three large tins of special SMA milk powder, Tablets, and a large box of rectal Valium ampules that is a first.

The hospital pharmacy has drawn up a prescription for a further six tins of SMA milk powder these will arrive by special currier in the next day or so, finding space to store more items that is going to be fun. An appointment to visit the GP has been arranged for next week, no idea why; might be a follow up from this hospital admittance. It is fantastic home again first things first cup of coffee and tea and preparation of Amanda's milk must be done, we have purchase four brand new bottles on the way home as some had become stained no amount of boiling or soaking improved the hygiene, so we replaced them. Amanda has had several fantastic days now, and this has enabled us to relax more taking the opportunity to take days out with friends.

Tomorrow, we have arranged a group day trip to Hunstanton just up the coast, there is an invite to a birthday party on Sunday at 3 pm being held at the disability Hall across the road from the Lowestoft Library looking forward to that. All being well next Monday we will be having a large beach party next to the Claremont Pier, but that is weather permitting naturally. We have just had a visit from the District Housing Office with an update on their proposed plans to improve our bungalow to accommodate Amanda's needs, they wanted to arrange a visit for twelve thirty on Friday next week "fine with us" I said "we are planning a trip to Yarmouth with friends at 2 pm."

The doorbell rang it was the social workers and health worker, "wow we are extremely popular today" I said, "we were just passing and thought we would pop in and check on things" they said. One hour and three cups of tea later the real reason for their visit came out, once again, the planning committee had met and decided again it was too costly all Government funding had been removed and there was no available grant money to do the required improvement work. This was the true reason for their visit but we did have a heart-to-heart discussion regarding Amanda's future needs and requirements which included our needs as a family. We were to say the least upset and pointed out broken promises by the authority to be honest I had to remind the social workers in no uncertain terms that it was the council who approached us, asking if we still wanted the work done.

I have become so angry; one moment it is on; the next it is off, "Why? Oh Why? Do they continue to give us false hope and then dash them shortly after? My hand was forced, and I made my feelings known, it was not because of grants but totally down to the issue that this is because I own the bungalow. Enough was enough clearly refusal of planning permission being down to that fact, why else are we being refused. Clearly for us it has become frustratingly unacceptable to allow this type of on then off excuse as to why it cannot be brought to some conclusion, "Simply build us a bungalow and we can sell up. problem solved or at least that is what I thought").

"No!" this was another issue preventing a decision to take on the next step, before I had finished my recommendation the Officers jumped in with the excuse they have no bungalows available, now that statement clearly was a foolish remark, quickly my anger had reached explosion point. ("Why are you lying?") "I know that the authority has Seven; yes, Seven bungalows at various stages of build in Fairfield Road" "Why can we not have one of them?" I by this Time had totally lost it clenching my fists, I was a close to swinging for someone if it was not for Yvonne, I may well have struck someone and certainly, would face assault charges.

That show of anger could well have damaged any chance of being considered for any form of help, I really messed up and called the Council housing office to apologise unfortunately I was unable to speak with any of the offers concerned. Three weeks passed and I was slightly taken aback when the senior housing officer telephone me requesting I meet up with him for a coffee and a chat at Ten o'clock Monday in his office, expecting the worse I agreed it would at least enable me if nothing else to apologise for my embarrassing and threatening outburst three weeks or so back.

I recall it was very bright and sunny Monday morning, I arrived outside the Offices fifteen minutes before Ten. Reluctantly a feeling of apprehension ranThrough my body like that of attending a job interview, I have never been one for nerves but did manage to bury them deep as I walked through the front door. After introducing myself to the receptionist, a door opened, and I was taken upstairs by a young lady to the office of the senior Housing Officer Robert and whose last name escape's me now. He was a small statured man in his mid to late thirties, he wore turtle shell framed glasses that remained attached to his forehead for the whole meeting.

The Coffee arrived in a large stainless steel coffee pot with two wide rim cups on saucers, several packets of assorted biscuits placed on a China plate and followed by a China milk jug. The loud sound of traffic outside the window made it a little difficult to hear what was being spoken so Robert closed it.

"Mr Cherry thank you for agreeing to meet me," he said "I have been following your family housing issue and would like to apologise for the misunderstanding throughout your case." Boy that knocked the wind out of my sail's I should be apologising to him not the other way round.

With the niceties over I was asked about my feelings and see if bridges might be built over our differences, "some work needed there" I said but finding common ground was I found out really was not that difficult. Again, in hindsight we both needed an acceptable outcome, talking it out in an adult grown up way was certainly the right way to proceed. I did have anger issues and this over the last few years had done more damage than good, I think it might have been Robert's calm approach and his ability to listen that I reacted too. We spoke a lot about the problems Amanda had and the effect that it had not just on me and the family but also on the needs that had been pointed out to us over the past couple of years. Set back after set back, broken promises, misleading statements saying one thing and smashing everyone's hope weeks down the line. I used the example of improvements to our bungalow, the fact it cost a substantial amount of out lay to have plans drawn up and submitted for planning permission finances which we could ill afford. Then told the permission had been refused, also the authority had been given government grants to carry out this type of work. The only person who was being punished was Amanda a young child who had been diagnosed as termly ill, we cry every night not knowing if or when she might pass-away.

It was the final nail in the coffin after housing offices approached us to see if we were still interested in improvement work, the government we were told had again, made grants available but shortly afterwards this was taken away. I challenged it naturally and asked that we be given a disabled bungalow, "We do not and are not building disable bungalows currently" unquote! It was that statement from an incompetent officer that caused me to blow my top, I knew that the authority has been building seven two/three-bedroom bungalow's for disable tenants in Fairfield Road so why did she lie?

Robert was rather taken back by the statement I had made and said he would look into that, he did concur that bungalows were being built and he would see what information he could sort out. I think he was rather stuck for words but he at least did listen which you know not everyone can do, let's see what comes of our heart-to-heart conversation later? Three weeks later, Yvonne and I were having a cup of tea. Amanda had been fed dressed and waiting to go out, we we're going to have day out in Hunstanton just up the coast with eight very close friends who have children with various degrease of disability some are blind; deaf. I many cases suffering mild or severe forms of spasticity and downs syndrome each family?

Each one of those families have a moving story to tell, stories that would chill the heart of those listening. At this point I am compelled to say, not a single parent would change the love and dedication they have toward each one of them ill or not. I only wish with all my heart, Government's leaders: taxpayers could realise and accept that families like us are the forgotten heroes. "We are unpaid carers, carers who continue even to this day to save the Government millions and millions of pounds a year and for what?" "Only to be continually challenged year on year, justifying to authorities that we still remain entitled to the measly pittance of benefits they pay." There I've had my rant, it isn't going to change any time soon."

"Where was I before I went off on one," "Oh yes as we struggled to get out of the narrow front door and were met by the postman." "Good morning, Mr and Mrs Cherry" he remarked as he handed us five envelopes including a thick large brown one. "You're very popular today," I laughed and took them from him. "More bills I suspect, Postmen nearly always bring bad news and generally do" "Just to let you know Postie I can go off people very quickly you know!" he chuckled as he walked away. Being tight for time I threw the unopened mail on the unit in the living room, they're probably only usual bills anyway.

"What a wonderful day we have had!" Amanda has been brilliant not a single problem she ate all her dinner we prepared has drank well even managed to acquire a bit of colour in her cheeks, something rarely seen over past months. Even though we have had a fantastic time today there is nothing better than returning home, Amanda must have enjoyed herself as she had fallen asleep and remained like that till about six thirty just in time for tea.

I was proved right about the letters that came this morning most were bills, Water Authority, British Gas, a letter from Lowestoft's education department and a letter from the London's Great Ormond Street Hospital. That must be an appointment for Amanda, I may be wrong, but it looks like it. "Now for the large one!) "It was quite thick and puffy; I must admit I was quite intrigued to be fair on its contents." But due to the fact our minds were really on other things this morning, I was truly disinterested and did not give a second thought. "I opened the envelope and seeing its contents made me go week at the knees, "I don't believe it!" I cried out. Reading the letter kind of knocked the wind out of me, "Yvonne, the housing department have only gone and agreed to allocated us a bungalow on Fairfield Road." They have even sent us a printed copy of the floor plan as well, "Darling" I cried out "it's massive," they had only gone and knocked two bungalows into one. "We have also been invited to a viewing next week, and if we find it acceptable, we should be able to move in at the end of next month."

Chapter Twenty-Two

MOVING HOME

"The struggle we have had over the past two years or so, in respect of home. improvements to improve the quality of life for Amanda is now moving to the next stage. We are due to have a viewing of the new bungalow on Friday. afternoon at three o'clock so looking excitingly toward that, and then if we like it. the next step will to be to put our bungalow in Kirkley Run on the market. It seemed like a lifetime for Friday to arrive finally it is here, when we arrived, The housing officer architect and the builder met us.

We were shown round the outside, the garden was quite large and clayish. builder's rubbish mixed in. They had laid a small sized and I mean small patio of about Fifteen Slabs, I made the comment like "That is not big Amanda's. wheelchair will not fit." Dawn Pointon the housing officer was standing just. behind me and heard my remarks, snapping back she said "if you are not happy. "Mr. Cherry sir!" You really have a problem; we could always offer it to someone else, you are lucky to have been. given first refusal we do have others wanting a bungalow like this!"

"I could have responded but remained calm" she has since the day we first met. had an issue with me, but again I put it down to her time of month. I certainly had no intention of affording her the pleasure of taking this bungalow away from us, And any way we have been waiting for this or something other far too long. Then came the opportunity to view the inside of the bungalow, well it was like a palace the place was massive. As you walked through the front door ahead of us was the first bedroom about twelve feet by eight foot six, as you came out of the bedroom a wide corridor just over three feet wide. To your left was a bathroom a very dark room due to the fact there was no window, "can I have a window put in?" I asked. Mrs Pointon again snap at me saying "No! this was the design of the building and cannot be changed," "It would just take an electric power cutter to put a window in the wall."

Well, you should have seen Mrs Pointon's face it was a picture to behold, her eyelids cringed; her top lip raised slightly; showing a section of her teeth and her bottom lip I swear began quivering. Any way I was told that the builder would cut a window in the wall to allow natural light to entre, there was also a large heavy changing table that folded up to the wall and as for the bath it was massive both deep and wide. A section of wall had been removed to allow a hoist to be installed, opposite the bathroom was extra-large bedroom this would be where Amanda slept. It was also equipped with patio doors to allow access to the patio and garden, next to that was our bedroom again quite spacious.

The largest room in the bungalow naturally was the Living room it must have been well over twenty feet by nineteen feet, I could have parked my Rover car in it and still had room to spare. The kitchen and the toilet were much larger than what we were used to in our own bungalow which was great. Three weeks after the visit to the new bungalow we received a telephone call, I remember it well as it had been pouring with rain over night with a violent thunderstorm. The call was from the housing department to tell us we could pick up the key for the new bungalow, sadly because of the weather we were unable to go and collect them. You can imagine how disappointed we were, but there was always tomorrow.

The timing of this call could not have come at a better time, as fifteen minutes later we received another call this time from our estate agent informing us that we had a buyer for our bungalow. Better still it was for Three thousand pounds over the asking price of twenty-eight thousand, I could hardly believe what was being told; what I did not know the buyers had been gazumped twice and were not prepared to let it happen a third time. I am pleased to say we had not been sitting on our backsides doing nothing but had started packing so the majority of our personal items were in crates in the front room, it was only the heavy items that needed wrapping up fridge, washing machine cupboards freezer etc.

We were unable to have a professional removing company, so to save money we had a one of our Citizen Band radio friends to help. He works for the fat and bone company driving a large lorry, it would take everything in two trips. Well, I think we should have contacted a removal firm, the lorry stunk of rotten meat but so strong even though he assured me he had steam cleaned it the day before. All the soft furnishings such as clothing, bedlinen, settee, chairs etc became impregnated with the strong sickening smell of rotten meat.

I am pleased that the move was only a mile away, it could well have been worse. After six cans of aerosol later the smell became more tolerable and after a few days had totally diminished, it took us about three weeks to settle in properly. Amanda remained quite well for almost two months after moving in but then thing began to happen, she began to fit quite violently at about three in the morning. I called for the doctor, who arrived fifteen minutes after putting the phone down, Dr. Stansfield a young man in I would say mid-twenties still a little inexperienced. I say that because of the fear in his eyes as he laid eyes on Amanda in a full flung seizure, and for the first time I watched a male doctor's face as tears ran down his cheeks.

He checked Amanda over; I could see he was really having difficulties but gave her a large rectal Valium. It was quite an ordeal for him and a strong cup of tea was called for, he remained with her till the effect of the Valium had fully taken hold. We sat in the front room and discussed with Dr. Stansfield Amanda's history of problems, all the things we must do, all the things we have done as well as the difficulty in getting doctors to listen to what we are saying. Naturally, he agreed with us on many things but admitted that he could not comment on the medical side of known difficulties that plague the NHS, but as one of its active clinicians they are doing their best. It was a whole ninety minutes before he was happy with Amanda's condition, if there was any change we were to call for an ambulance. Amanda slept ok, but then she would, seeing she had received ten milligrams of rectal Valium, she was very stiff in her limbs and felt as if she was a curled-up piece of wood.

"I remember somewhere in the back of my mind" being told a hot bath can be quite relaxing, so I decided to give it a try. Filling the pool size bath and I assure you I'm not joking it was massive God knows what my water bill will be, still I had it almost half full and hot the bathroom was full of steam. I got in and thenYvonne passed Amanda to me, in an instant Amanda began to loosen up and in three minutes she had become floppy. Even the slight twitching seemed to disappear and Yvonne remarked she has fallen asleep, we could have cried as she lay in my arms so relaxed I swear she even began snoring. Lowering the changing table boy that was heavy Yvonne took Amanda off me, she was quite pink looking even her face looked flush. Maybe the water was a little too hot but as she did not scream or cry, I think it worked well.

Amanda was dresses in a red floral dress with a white frilly border and puffed short sleeves, she ate all her ready break breakfast and drank a bottle of her special milk tinted with a cup of tea. She enjoyed it and then had a nap for half an hour, the pink colour vanished quite quickly and her relaxed muscles became rigid once more. We had a few bits to unpack in her bedroom and to find a home for but because the day was looking good, we decided to take Amanda to Nicholas Everett Park to feed the ducks. The fresh air would do us all some good, plus we had half a loaf of mouldy bread to get rid of. The duck really did not get much as the large swans got into the act and bullied the duck away, so we did throw some on the ground and the ducks flew up and got some after all. Dark clouds began to appear over the beach and heading our way, I had no intension of being caught in the storm that was about to hit us.Still, we have been out for over two hours, so it is time we got home, I think.

We only just made it home, suddenly there was a loud clash of thunder right over the top of us and a flash of lightning. Then the heavens opened it slung it down so hard our drains were only just able to take the water build up. We thought it might even come in the front door, but as quickly as it came the rain stopped and the sun came out to reveal the most vivid rainbow one could ever surmise it was beautiful so, so beautiful. Things were about to change and change they did, the phone rang, and social services wanted to see us Monday morning at ten o'clock to discuss the matter of respite. What we were not aware off was what the discussion would cover, but that was to change on Monday morning.

The doorbell rang dead on ten o'clock and there were three female officers all carrying black briefcases; two dressed in dark grey jackets one with a stripped knee length skirt and black stockings, another had a clean white shirt with a very thin bowtie that blew in the wind black trousers and black shoes. As for the third she was wearing a bright red open necked blouse a long-pleated flowing below the knees dress and dark red shoes, each had a different hair style one whose hair was black was like a bob the second had fair hair and the one who was wearing the dress had exceptionally long blond hair pinned back with a yellow ribbon and laid over her left shoulder.

Life was about to change dramatically for both Amanda and for us, as a whole family and I was not sure if it was going to be something enjoyable.The reason for their visit was to discuss Amanda's educational needs as well as our right to receiving respite from twenty-four seven care, like most things in life local authorities do a great deal of making decisions about people behind their backs. Sometimes for the betterment of families and debatably sometimes not so beneficial, but today these officers came to propose that we consider enrolling Amanda in Warren Special school on the Beccles Road. Apparently as Amanda is just shy of her fifth birthday the new term at Warren begins in September only two months away, it would be great if she could start now and see how she would get on. Also, it will allow the staff to assess Amanda's personal needs.

Naturally, this was not even on our radar and if I'm honest is the last thing on our minds. This moment in time is one of the hardest days in most parents Calendar lives, a time when for the first your child is separated from your five year protection suddenly comes to an end. Made even more poignant due to her medical issues. Every day we know is going to be an anxious day for us both, if she starts having major seizures, will they be able to control them? How will the other children react to her? Our worries about education, is it the right thing for Amanda due to her medical condition and why may I ask; would we want to send her to school? We found it quite baffling to say the least, "Although we agree educationally there is no chance Amanda would benefit from schooling." The benefits would come in the form of a more structured physiotherapy regime and clearly in their opinion she might not get we're she to remain at home" said one of the officers"

"When are we looking to begin her schooling"? I asked, "Non like the present came back the answer. They were not going to waste time in getting the ball rolling, we anticipated the possibility of both you and Mrs Cherry agreeing so we have arranged it with Warren School and are expecting her to attend school on Monday. A taxi has been booked to pick her up with an escort at eight-twenty-five, and will bring her home at about four o'clock. "Were you trying to impress us or something with precise timings" I asked flippantly.

Life as we know it was going to dramatically change, the fear of the unknown has now come to the fore. Fear of no longer being able to monitor closely any changes which are so minuscule at times and could be easily missed by an untrained eye. If when she starts fitting to be able to distinguish when one seizure ends and another starts, and the importance of keeping a record of them for the hospital records which we as well keep as back up.

Chapter Twenty-Three

STARTING
SCHOOL

Date Monday fifteenth of August nineteen eighty-three, another date deeply edged on our minds. Half an hour from now Amanda is being collected by a taxi and transported to the Warren Special School just down the road from us. A real mixed cocktail of feeling is running through my stomach as the wall clock races toward eight-forty-three, Amanda has had a bowel of Wheat-a-bisk for her breakfast a cup of tea and is now sitting in her chair with her coat on ready to go.

True to their word a taxi arrived seconds before the clock hit eight-forty-three, we did shed a tear as the taxi made off with Amanda. Four a clock cannot come quick enough and the of the anxiety we both had made the day seem a great deal longer, we phoned several times throughout the day to ask how she was and each time were assured she was doing fine, and she would be home at four. It felt like four o'clock was never going to arrive, after all we did spend most of the afternoon clock watching. "The old saying a watched Kettle" sort of sprung to mind, Amanda returned shortly after four o'clock and she was sound asleep.

"Amanda's school bag was full of paintings, paintings of her feet and hands That had been dipped in paint green feet and yellow hands. Also tucked neatly in the back of her chair, we found a report book, explaining what they had been doing with Amanda and how she has been throughout the day. The teachers also enclosed with the report book a letter asking if we could also write how she had been while at home and give them a heads up if she has been having seizures or eating issues while at home. Yvonne and I could not see anything wrong with that request and would have done that anyway, we also sent daily medication as matter of course not there was a lot just a couple of tablets and her Phenergan anti-convulsant mixture.

As we had concerns about Amanda, or should I say strong attachment issues we were given an open-door agreement, what I mean by that is if we have any worries or doubts we could visit the school at any time. As you might guess we did act upon it quite a lot especially if she had not been too good at home (hence the report book). We also will ensure that we continue to include at least two changes of clothing, as she re-turned home today wearing different clothes from what we sent her to school in.

With the arrival of the school's summer holidays we were more relaxed in ourselves and have planned a trip down to Oxfordshire, and we have a hospital appointment at Great Ormond Street for an annual check-up. Almost forgot that we must keep the consultants up to speed, I do not drive down to London anymore as drivers down there are mental and I speak from experience ("Frightening") at the best of times. So, we have been taking the train, it means a six fifty early departure from Lowestoft to arrive at Liverpool Street station by ten fifty, we had to stop several times to allow the people to get off and more importantly during the week school children as well at Ipswich for about five minutes so that another train can couple up on the back.

We are un-able to use the underground as Amanda is in her wheelchair, so instead, we took a taxi or as they call them in London a "Black Cab." Traffic was horrendous and every traffic light was against us, the old taxi clock metre seemed to change second by second even when we had stopped. We eventually pulled into Great Ormond Street Hospital some twenty-eight minutes later, thinking the clock would stop, "did its hell!" it just had to click over one more time. Seven pounds thirty-six pence and still believe it or not the flaming driver expected a tip, so I rounded it up to seven pounds and forty pence in small change.

With my pockets truly empty of heavy coins I was able to enter the hospital with a spring in my step, we had over an hour and a half to wait before it was time for Amanda's appointment so we decided to get something to eat from the hospital canteen. Amanda was ok as we prepared her food before we left home, boy what a shock it cost almost ten pounds to buy one cup of tea one bottle of coke and two readymade ham sandwiches. "Boy, don't they know how to charge!" As per usual the clinic was running slightly late, too many coffee breaks "me thinks!" anyway eventually Amanda's name was called and the time was almost two thirty pm. Yvonne and I were bombarded with so many questions regarding her well-being, they were pleased to hear her seizures had also reduced the stiffening in her arms and legs were a little more supple.

Amanda was beginning to become restless, the clinic lasted just under twelve minutes and at no time did the consultant take Amanda out of her wheelchair. I was rather disappointed as we did ask if he going to physically examine her, but he said he was quite happy to leave her in her chair. When we had attended appointments in the past Amanda were always taken out of her chair and physically examined, but for some reason this time the consultant refused. We thought this clinic was a real waste of time, after four-and-a-half-hour train journey an expensive taxi ride, extortionate cost of food and a clinic running late proved to be a complete and utter waste of time.

On our homeward journey we had plenty of time to deliberate on the events of the day, as you may well imagine there was a great deal to discuss. This will Naturally not happen in future as we will ensure Amanda is taken out of her chair long before her clinic appointment, it was close to nine o'clock in the evening when we reached our front door Amanda was sound asleep and rather than disturb her we put her to bed fully clothed. All Yvonne and I wanted was a cup of tea and coffee put our feet up and relax for a little while. The events of the day still played on our minds; the discussion again made us start analysing what had happened, and the more we analysed the angrier we became not a good thing I think just before going to bed ourselves.

Amanda must have had quite a tiring day yesterday as she slept till ten am, it was also an extremely hot summers day forcing us to have all the windows and open to allow the cool breeze to pass through the bungalow. We plan to drive to Sheringham tomorrow, and then on Thursday we plan to visit Hunstanton, with a group of families who like us have children and young adult with mental and physical disabilities. We hire a coach, and they take us to various destinations and then at the end of the day return us to the disabled club in Till Road Lowestoft around Seven pm.

So, today we plan to remain at home, I have the small inflatable pool out and this being brand new was difficult to get out of the box. The next thing was trying to blow it up, is took ages and even made my chest hurt ("get a pump next time me thinks!"). Connecting the hose pipe to the bathroom tap had its problems but managed it in the end, filling it up with water seemed to take ages only to find I had over filled it and that alone will teach me for not keeping an eye on it. Testing the water, I was shocked how cold it felt literally freezing, so I'll allow the sun to warm it up.

Amanda was very thirsty when she woke up, and rather hungry as she literally woofed down her ready break. Yvonne dressed Amanda in a pale blue summer dress with short puffy sleeves, and to avoid any sun burn we slapped on strong Sun Cream. The day was peaceful, no visitor's the sound of the radio playing a mixture of 40's and sixties music quietly in the background. Strange collection I agree but there is a lot to say about nostalgia, for me it is being able to hear the words of any song; not struggling to catch the words of today's music that is bashed out. School holidays over we prepare to send Amanda back to School, it had to happen Amanda had an unbelievably bad night last night. For some reason her temperature soared to 42 degrees Celsius, naturally panic set in, so we called the doctor who arrived 15 minutes later. Yvonne had stripped all her night clothes of and she had begun patting her down with cool water, she started having the strongest seizures for nearly 6 weeks. She presented with a new problem projectile vomiting she even got the doctor; he wasted no time in calling an ambulance as she was really in a bad way.

The ambulance arrived within 9 minutes but were unable to stabilize her for at least 30 minutes. Yvonne and I were a jabbering mess we each thought is this it, is she finally going to succumb to the power of the seizures? Panic again starts to sets in, and as usual the instructions from the mouths of those working on Amanda "We're going to sort her out she'll be fine" never gives a sense of calm, we have been living with this for over 5 years. You would think by now we would be used to the seizures; well, you'd be very much mistaken there is always a slight difference; a real quirkiness we would say to each episode. Yvonne and I can never be sure what type of episode she is going to present us with, but we have learnt if nothing else expect the unexpected and that is the frightening thing about this whole thing.

It was almost a full forty minutes before the Ambulance crew were happy to move Amanda to the Ambulance and transport her to hospital, it is never an easy thing to achieve. I arrived on the Children's ward only to be asked to wait as the duty paediatrician was finishing attaching an I.V drip, then explaining to us that Amanda may have caught a bug and anti-biotics are being given via the drip. We stayed only for an hour; Amanda had started to calm down there was not a lot we could do as the hospital staff as usual had everything under control, Yvonne and I left for home and would return tomorrow at 7.30am.

On our return we were told that Amanda had a rather unsettled night and the night staff had just finished their hand over, Amanda was allocated a young 23-year-old student nurse by the name of

Sandra Webster. I'm sure these nurses get younger and younger each time we see them, as always on entering Amanda's cubicle after kissing her good morning I made my way to the bottom of her cot and peeked at her charts. She had a raised temperature of almost 39.7 degrees and her pulse rate up, can never understand how they work out the hart beat over or under the pulse rate.

Amanda was kept in hospital for two weeks, whatever the bug was that caused this episode I am not able to say. As normal a record is kept of her seizures, three hundred and twenty-six in total since admittance and 74 before she was brought into hospital making a total of 1,437.267. I think I have said this before I'm not too sure if it is a good thing to know how many seizures, she has suffered. We have noticed that just lately we have become somewhat of a sounding board again in the ward, disgruntled parents have been asking us for advice: advice on how to complain about the treatment by doctor Back. They have unfortunately been around when I have an argument mainly in Amanda's cubicle or quite often at the nurse's station, so in a way I have made a rod for my own back. "I'm really unqualified to give advice" I said as parents if you are worried, concerned or not happy with the treatment being given then bring it up with the paediatrician to explain why they are doing what they are doing.

Mr Cherry you and your wife are always on the ward when your daughter is in, and you see more of what's going on than we! "This is a fair point, but I have no authority to challenge any other medical actions taken by the doctors." It turns out that they are fearful of reprisals be taken against their child. "Ah I know exactly where you're coming from!" As I am so they say already speaking out over the treatment or lack of treatment given to Amanda, I am already in doctor Back's bad books and openly in front of everyone tell him what you think.

Fighting on behalf of others was not something I was able to agree, I would though watch for problems and report it to the parents when next I saw them. I am not that much of an ogre, little did I know that there would be a problem arise that very evening. Yvonne and I were about to go home at nine thirty in the evening, when one of the nurses we noticed was giving an orange drink to a little girl I'll call her "Shannon" I think to protect her identity. Shannon and her parents arrived the same time as Amanda, we instantly clicked and spoke constantly and became I believe good friends. As we passed the nurse's station, I pointed out to the staff nurse that the nurse was giving Shannon a drink of orange juice, I recall Shannon's mum telling the admission doctor that Shannon cannot drink anything with orange in it. Shannon would suffer an Anaphylactic reaction, naturally we continued going home thinking the staff nurse would stop the nurse from giving the drink.

What Yvonne and I did not know at the time was all hell let loose, when we arrived the next morning, we were informed that Shannon had passed away about the same time as we were driving out of the hospital car park. What made it even disturbing was that Shannon's parents did not get to the hospital until 30 minutes after she passed, both Yvonne and I were devastated all the staff on the wards are clearly so upset. What Yvonne and I witnessed as we left the ward last night Shannon being given a drink of orange, may well have been the cause of her death. Yet again hindsight has played its merciless reminder to the fact of how fragile life can be, Mark and Ann "sorry I forgot to introduce them into the story they are the parents of Shannon. Like us they are young parents of two girls Shannon being the younger sibling, they were still on the ward unable to leave the lifeless body of Shannon. No amount of consoling can take away the pain of losing someone, I know I have experienced that pain. It upset me so much I decided there and then to make myself available and become a spokesperson for parents who request it, there were too many problems occurring and going unchallenged it is time to try and nip things-in-the-bud and take on board many of the concerns parents' kind of bottled up.

After the trauma of last week, we were informed Amanda will be able to return home and a final check by doctor Back on Friday will be discharged, obviously, they are discharging to have a week-end clear of nonurgent patients. On Tuesday Amanda has another hospital routine appointment I asked if she will need to attend as she is being discharge Friday, the ward sister said she would enquire for me, but it is more likely they will cancel the appointment.

"I've said it before and I'll say it again, doctor Back and his team have a great deal to answer for. Unfortunately, the hospital administration and this is only my opinion remember are failing his patients daily, how many more patients will be put at risk as Shannon last week. Amanda has now been out of hospital for 13 weeks and has had a good seizure free period, her hospital appointments and results have been positively encouraging. Naturally, we keep taking our own weekly records to hand over at each of her hospital appointment for inclusion of their records, hopefully they do keep them but not sure they are certainly acceptable at the time.

Another milestone is approaching fast Amanda's nineth Birthday which is just three weeks away, we have a lot of planning to do in the meantime and we are unsure at this moment when, where to celebrate it. Yvonne's mum has offered to bake her a cake, I did have a little disagreement with her as I was going to have it made professionally in town. I wish I had kept my mouth shut as it was not worth the backlash, for even thinking of it not just from Yvonne's mum but her sisters too. (in-laws eh!).

"Happy Birthday to you; Happy Birthday to you; Happy Birthday dear Amanda, Happy Birthday to you!" "WOW!! 9 years old today, I don't think anyone knows the feeling both Yvonne and I have today." The prognosis from doctor Back 9 years ago was, and I quote "Amanda's life expectancy would in his opinion be 2 – 8 years tops," boy was he so thankfully wrong. It has not been easy we'll admit, we've had many challenges to face on the way. Battles with authorities, hospitals, including one time with "GOD all mighty" mostly though with Amanda herself. The fear of losing her at any time over the past 9 years has taken its toll on our mental and physical health, and to be honest she has had episodes on more than one occasion Gt. Ormond Street I recall. Sometime after that episode Yvonne and I were informed of many other occasions, but you know after all that we have had an awfully close supportive family who also have remained a solid wall around us. Anne-marie her sister has suffered more than any of us, she has to some extent lost a lot of her childhood and in a large way been unintentionally push to one side.

It goes without saying that we have neglected her upbringing dramatically if it We're not for Yvonne's mum and dad taking her under their wing we could now be experiencing a total alienated child. A child with serious issues around stability, but obviously Anne – marie had realised why she is where she is. We put her understanding of the situation down to her nan and grandad, again that shows the closeness of true family life.

Chapter Twenty-Four

A CHANGE OF AMANDA'S PAEDIATRICIAN

A manda true to form remained seizure free till the New Year 1983 January 1st to be exact at 4.30pm, Amanda began to have seizures to the like we have not seen for a long while. We phoned as usual for an Ambulance, and it arrived in about 10 minutes, in that ten minute she had 15 gran – mal seizures, she was bleeding from the mouth and mixed with froth. The Ambulance Paramedics bless them; tried to stop us from panicking, by saying it is likely Amanda has bitten her tongue or cheek and that is the reason for the bleeding. Controlling the seizure was getting us up tight, even the Paramedics were frustrated and could only administer a certain amount of sedation and they had reached that level. It took more than 30 minutes before Amanda began to calm, it had clearly taken its toll on the medics and Yvonne and me.

Eventually we arrived on the children's ward, the seriousness was high, and we were taken to the family waiting room. Jenny Roberts the ward sister brought us both a cup of tea and biscuits, "Doctors are with Amanda and are trying desperately to bring her seizures under control." She said "I'll come and speak to you as soon as I can." Clearly tears were rolling down our cheeks, it has been an exceptionally long time since Amanda has shown this power of seizures. In fact being truthful, we have not seen these since she first had them 9 years ago. So, you can imagine controlling them can be enormously difficult, remembering how we were when she first was inflicted with these seizures the constant anger and frustration screams out enough is enough. That same anger and frustration is affecting my mental state, questions on why Amanda is still suffering, which manifests in my constant public arguments between me and doctor Back. The outcome of those altercations between us goes to explain in someway why I decided to eventually to help with the problems other parents we're facing on the ward.

Unfortunately, it was clear to staff members that they were looking at a serious case of personalities, "(remember Amanda is my child and I will rightly or wrongly fight tooth and nail to get her the essential medical care she is entitled too)" Today being a Friday is an especially important day, it's the regular doctors ward rounds. This is where the inform us of the complex medical successes or failures of the week just past, Normally the latter in Amanda's case. There was a notable aroma (smell) of Paraldehyde in the outside corridors, long before we turned the corner for the Ward. It may well have been administered in the last half hour or so, and "Yes!" it was from Amanda's cubical. Last night Amanda had been uncontrollably fitting and biting her lips tongue and cheeks, all had been bleeding somewhat and were left with no alternative but to take the action of Paraldehyde.

Amanda was really looking pale not her normal skin colourisation, around her eyelids a dark appearance with some redness showing in the corners of her eyes including her lips. We had the feeling that a great deal more had gone on than we were being told; I have never seen Amanda in this light before. Strong feeling of fear and anxiety took hold and as the tears rolled down our faces, I totally lost control panic kicked in I began shouting out "Where is doctor Back?" "Why is he not here?" I found myself being physically restrained from Amanda's cubical pushed and dragged to the parents waiting room, it took four male nurses to manhandle into the room and watched over me till I eventually calmed down enough and become more Civilised. By the time I was eventually allowed to make my way into Amanda's cubical doctor Back had left the ward, that again will teach me not to fly off the handle and to think before I act. Thinking about it; I wonder if he had been made aware that I was coming in and seeing Amanda's condition would send me ballistic, so it looks as if steps have been taken should I arrive while he was on his rounds and having to face me and my verbal attacks on him.

The main thing on my mind now is getting back to Amanda who by the way was still fitting even though she had paraldehyde, her poor little legs were so bruised and soar looking it brought tears to our eyes. I had now the chance to view her medical charts at the bottom of her cot, she has really been put through the grinder bless her. We again asked why we had not been called and put in the picture of this latest episode, it would not have been such a shock for us walking in on the procedures. Looking at the charts Amanda's vital signs showed that her BP and Temp were quite elevated, that may explain why it was proving such a problem controlling the seizures. 722 registered seizures were recorded before all hell let loose, so I would strongly suggest there are more than a few seizures missed off. Gillian a close friend of ours has finally completed typing out Amanda's diary, I dare not tell her I have another 7 books to type up I think I'll do them myself when I get the chance.

It was 6.30 pm when we decided to go home, the events of the day has really taken it out on us, Amanda has not been good all day and on edge even with the sedation. Her left arm has been continually twitching and her breathing also appeared a little laboured, even when placed on her back or propped up with the V-shape pillow. Staff nurse Francis Monro said they might give her a nebuliser, but will see how she is later. Seven o'clock the night staff come on duty and at the meeting before the shift change, they'll be made aware of how Amanda has been today.

Yvonne and I got to the hospital early but not nearly enough as the night staff had gone, Sister Katherine Paker was on duty today and she entered the room and informed us that last night was not a good one, quite upsetting for a couple of new nursing staff members in fact. Amanda began fitting again at 8.30 pm and she said the night staff counted 78 but then at around 10.15 pm she again began to stiffen up, her left arm became very stiff head twisted back and face became distorted eye rolled back and grinding of gums as well as moaning. It was impossible to open her up, each seizure lasting ten minutes. Amanda so Sister Parker said entered a violent jerking phase, not wanting to experience yesterday night's episode to happen again called for the duty paediatrician.

He was horrified with what he was witnessing as he walk into the room, so phased out was he wrote up for some rectal Valium to see if that would calm her down. After 20 minutes Amanda was still in status, and frustration started to take hold of the doctor and nursing staff. Paraldehyde being the final option 2 of the nurses became so emotional they had to leave the room, it's a procedure that would upset some people seeing it for the first time. Because it is an oil-based drug it can only be used / administered with a glass syringe and a large size needle, it then must be pushed into the muscle of the leg. Not an easy thing to do at the best of time, Yvonne and I always leave the room if there. Once given it forms a lump and until it disperses over a brief period and still leaving a hole where the needle penetrated.

I understand that Amanda was hooked up to an IV drip as in his opinion Amanda's little body has undergone enough injections for one day, He wrote a note for doctor Back to check on her when he comes in today as he was truly not happy with her condition when he saw her. One will not know just how I am feeling to have another doctor raise concerns over Amanda's condition, I just wish they could verbally express it in public. I know it is professional ethics and all that, but it is a dream I have on being open and honest with everything.

It was around 4.30 pm doctor Back graced us with his presence and then totally blank Yvonne and me as he walked into Amanda's room, it just shows you how ignorant and pig headed the man is. I have never been one to tolerate this sort of behaviour from anyone and I certainly do not intend to start now, as doctor Back left the room, I followed quickly behind him and as he paused at the nurse's station, I let him know just how I felt regarding the ignorance he just now showed blanking both Yvonne and I as if we were not there. "Doctor Back. Sir trying to keep as calm as I could, I am aware of the fact we do not much like each other but what you just did has now been seen by others and shows everyone just how ignorant you are and clearly justifies as well as supports the anger and contempt I have for you," I said. "You were left a letter by the doctor who attended Amanda last night, and it I understand explained to you his concerns over Amanda informing you of the action he had to take to try and bring Amanda's seizures to an end." "Yet at no time while in Amanda's room did you

- Either acknowledge we were in the room.
- Physically examine or touch Amanda
- Raised the issue of the past 48 hours.
- Nor did you look at her medical notes at the bottom of her cot.

I by this time was getting more and more up tight, I really was struggling not to loose it and the nursing staff could see that. The veins in my neck felt as if they we're going to explode and as for my hands they are eager to lash out given half the chance. 48 hours ago, I understand there was an issue you failed to tell us where Amanda required resuscitation, I am aware this has happened several times over the years. I have witnessed it while Amanda was in Gt Ormond Street, do you not think we should not have been told or do you think you're God?

It now worries me; "I ask myself how many other patients you over the years have you treated the same way?" it was at that point I must have hit a nerve he turned and faced me his face and neck look strawberry red; eyes almost popping out and angrily snapped back. "If I were you Mr. Cherry!" I'd advise you to watch what you say in public, I snapped back and said "it is only my opinion but it appears that you have a problem with children who have mental or physical issues." The example I use clearly in my opinion has been his attitude over eight/nine years ago, when first he met Amanda and his advice was, we should leave Amanda in hospital and to go home and forget we ever had her. It was as that point something snapped inside, "your credibility sunk lower that of a gutter rat." I said "That along with your delays in getting the right medical attention needed has placed her where she is today, it was also a statement made by Consultants at Gt. Ormond Street who could not understand why you; yes, you doctor Back did not make the referral for urgent admission after 4 weeks.

It might never have prevented today's diagnosis, but it certainly could well have reduced the damage we now have. "Mr. Cherry!" "You have had several second opinions, Norfolk and Norwich NHS, Cambridge NHS, to name a few." I could not argue with that fact, but what I could challenge was him sending his findings (reports) to back up everything he had done. They did not research their own conclusions. My continual challenges I was about to find out would come back and bit me on the backside, any smug feeling I may have had was wiped of my face. In an instant I understood the fears of other parents reluctance to challenge his competency, "Mr. Cherry; I am no longer going to going to put up with your critisisum or challenges, or the making of personel attacks on my medical computencies challenging my decision at every turn. I am not going to seek legal actions against you, but contrary to what you might think, I understand the anger and frustration you have regarding Amanda's diagnosis. I have many children coming to this and other hospitals with complicated issues some are easy and some like Amanda's are so problamatic we struggle to resolve the illness presented." he said "Therefore I am washing my hands of both you and Amanda I suggest you find someone else if you can to take you and Amanda on their books."

I could not believe what I was hearing, I know I have challenged a lot of his actions or should I say the lack of. But Amanda is our child and as a mother and father we expect the best, and nothing but the best. My brain was now in overdrive struggling to make sence of what has just occurred, Amanda is now without a qualified Paediatrician and it is all down to me and my fatherly pride. I have been told many times that one day my attitude will get me into trouble, well, it has now happened. Clearly in my opinion his action might be seen as a form of deriliction to his hypocratic oath, I feel that only God will judge that when the time comes.

What I was unaware of was the feelings of some nursing staff members, I found out shortly after doctor Back walked out supported many of the medical challenges I made. They said doctor Back could have handled it profesionally a great deal better, but agreed that in their opinion Amanda at times was given a raw deal. "Where do I go now?" I asked myself although I wished this outcome had not occurred we were where we where, I'll be honest I was seriously now panicing inside I urgently needed to find another doctor who was willing to put Amanda on their books. The enourmous fear I have is my reputation for being Confrontational and how badly that will bode with other practioners.

Not wanting to leave Amanda in a type of limbo, I was informed that a young doctor by the name of "Eric Patterson" was due to do his ward round sometime this afternoon. It seems that the nurses think he is the bee's kneese, they were quite sure I were to approach him and tell him what's happened may take Amanda on his books. Well it was not that easy as he was under some time Pressure, and flew past Amanda's room so fast I honestly managed to miss him. Luck was on my side as his personnal Secretary had to discuss several matters regarding one of his patience, Staff nurse "Lisa Black" called me over to have a word. "Cheryl Law this is Mr Cherry whom I spoke to you about just now," she said "I was wondering if you might be able to help him?" "Hello Mr Cherry!" she said "how might I help?" I explained the problem I have including briefly why I in the prodigamont I find myself, Amanda sadly has no paediatrician and at the moment is in quite a bad way. I know my actions have not been acceptable in many cases but the action of doctor Back punishing Amanda is in my opinion outragious, is there anyway you could on my behalf request doctor Patterson to take he on? I know it's a big ask, but please I'm desperate I really am. "I'll discuss your concerns and let you know."

Three days passed and we had not heard a thing, but unknown to us doctor Patterson had been to see Amanda several times. He I understand was not happy either with the treatment or the lack of that Amanda has had, according to the nurses he at one stage became quite emotional leaving her room to gain some composure. At least that was the opinion of the nursing staff. Amanda's condition dramtically improved by the end of the week and her seizures seem to have stopped, doctor Patterson came and saw us he told us he was really pleased with her progress.

Should Amanda remain seizure free for the next four days he sees no reason why she can't go home! Being told that was without doubt music to our ears I can tell you, "Thank you God; Thank you!"

Amanda must have been in a great deal of discomfort; both her thighs were badly bruised from the number of Paraldehyde injections. She also had a couple of lumps on both thighs these lumps were quite painful to touch, hopefully over time these will disappear or at least that is what we have been told. As we were giving Amanda a warm milky tea, a Doctor Martin Roberts popped into the room and gave us an update on Amanda's illness. Results of tests taken shows Amanda had somewhere picked up a nasty virus they are sure it was not in the hospital but could not rule it out confidently, test results now show she is clear, and Doctor Patterson is happy to discharge her on Tuesday Morning. Great news smiles all round and to show our feelings I will bring in a large tin of chocolates for the nursing staff, just to say thank you for the work they have done and for the support they gave me over the last few days.

We're going home today "Yahoo" could hardly control our emotions, as usual there was the delay waiting for her drugs to be sent from the pharmacy. Doctor Patterson came to say goodbye and give

Amanda a final check, he gave us a letter to take to Amanda's GP and an appointment to his clinic four weeks from now. "Our unconditional thanks to you doctor Patterson for taking Amanda on your books" I said "I really thought that my history would have gone against me; so, thank you!"

One might think four weeks was a long time, but I can assure you it flew past very quickly indeed. Due to heavy rain and traffic issues almost caused us to be late for Amanda's appointment, it also was unhelpful when it came to finding a car parking space. We arrived with minutes to spare before her name was called, in fact the nurse was still doing her weight and length checks. The examination room was quite full of medical practitioners, including social workers, physiotherapists ward sister and taking the minutes taking Cheryl Law doctor Patterson's personal secretary. Right in the middle of them was Doctor Patterson himself, everyman in the room including the physiotherapist were dressed to the nine light grey suits and ties. The ties were not coloured the same in fact, far from it a very deep red, blue with yellow stars I think and black with stripes.

"Please take a seat," Doctor Patterson said. The chair were well padded which made a change from the bucket type in the waiting room, Cheryl described a slimmed down version of the issues that Amanda had and the treatment we as a family had undergone over the years now she was a little agitated but not sure why. either she was hungry or tired well, she normally has a sleep around this time. So that could be the reason we were asked how Amanda has been since being discharged, "not too bad doctor Patterson." I replied "As you can see Amanda still has the nasty affects from the IV sights and the bruising plus lumps from the Paraldehyde injections, which for me are still a worry I will feel better when eventually, they disappear." "How has she been seizure wise?" "I am glad you asked Doctor Patterson!" "I'm pleased to say not a single seizure so far touching wood," as I said it. "Can you lay Amanda on the Couch so we can examine her? he said Everyone except Cheryl got up and stood around the couch, we were quite surprised as it has been a long time since we have seen this happen at a clinic. There was a great deal of talking, but their voices were Rather low and so only got the odd word or so. They spent a great deal of time examining her legs and arms, it must have been my statement of the bruising and lumps she had. After redressing her they sat down again, Tina Jones the social worker asked if we were receiving help with disposable nappies, we both in unison said NO!

Yvonne went on to say we have been asking many times if there was any chance of getting help with nappies, but the answer we kept getting was no not currently. "What!" she said "Right leave it with me I will get this matter sorted when I get back to the office, nappies are available. I am puzzled on why you are being told that they do not supply them.

Simon Clarke the occupational therapist through his examination said he was concerned that Amanda was presenting in his opinion some worrying posture issues, issues that in his opinion should be tackled urgently. He will contact us in a few days to try out some equipment, all this attention and concerns hit me emotionally but in an effective way to. Just look what Amanda has been missing all these years while under Doctor Back, questions that really should have been asked when first diagnosed. Everyone in this room could not believe either what they were seeing or in some cases what we were saying, I suppose it is now a case of treating Amanda and compiling a new file breaking down her personal needs not only physically but mentally too. Doctor Patterson and his colleagues would need to continue their discussions after we left, luckily Amanda was his last patient of the day.

The pulling about Amanda had today I think did not help, she began having a seizure session as we were going home in the car. I had to pull over in a lay-by To allow Yvonne to climb in the back so Yvonne could try and calm her down hopefully ("no chance"), the seizures lasted till about 9.45 pm when she fell sound asleep each seizure takes a lot out of her what makes it worse is that she is unable to eat or drink. In the last 3 hours Amanda has had a total of 273 seizures, we are not sure if that is the end of it as her eyes behind the lids are showing rapid movement. Rightly or wrongly, I do not class them as seizures I just don't know, over the last eight or nine months I have noticed this happening a great deal.

As promised the social worker Tina Jones telephoned to arrange a home visit for next Monday morning around 10 am, I told her that Amanda had not been too good since all the pulling about in the clinic but we are hoping she will be back at school next week so that should be fine. No sooner had I put the phone down when the front doorbell rang, it was the local pharmacist delivering a large box of Amanda's medication (mainly six large tins of powdered milk). I apologised to the pharmacist as I had totally forgotten to collect them from the chemist, that is what happens when you have other things spinning round your head.

Amanda thank God was well enough to go to school on Monday, although I did have my doubts at the time. If things go belly up, I informed the assistant that we would be available to bring her home. A flash of lightning and then a loud clash of thunder so powerful it made our windows shake; it went very dark and suddenly the heavens opened. The rain was so hard the droplets were bouncing of the road several inches high, we almost ended up being flooded as the drains struggled to cope. Thunder and lightning and heavy rain lasted 20 minutes, clouds parted the sun came out a rainbow appeared and within I don't know an hour; you would not have known it had rained. Tina arrived just before 12.15 pm and apologised for lateness, "I would have been here sooner but the rain was so heard it was difficult to see where one was going." She said I have also brought a colleague with me, this is Kay she is training to become a Social worker in Norfolk and Norwich hospital.

Tina was none too happy at the hospital clinic when we informed her that we have not been given help with the supply of disposable nappies, come to that equipment that might be of some help for Amanda. Today she came with a large box inside was 3 packs of nappies enough to see Amanda through at least a couple of months, "when these run out all we do is order another box" she said. Tina informed us that she has been in touch with social services department bosses enquiring about respite, I assume they thought it to be something to consider at some time. When asked my feelings and thoughts on the matter of respite I replied sharply over my dead body, I am not, nor will I ever allow someone else to look after Amanda. Amanda and I had a massively close bond between us, I promised myself I would never allow anyone to intentionally split us up.

Two weeks have passed since Tina had visited us, when I got a phone call from Simon Clarke the occupational therapist. He would like to see us On Wednesday afternoon at about 4 pm, he has a piece of equipment he wanted to try on Amanda. "Amanda should be home from school by then so fine" I said, all the shouting I have done regarding the type of therapy given to Amanda appears to have hit a nerve somewhere, so we are looking forward to his visit. We were hoping to go to Norwich today, but it was not to be. Amanda has been exceptionally well no problems, the bruising has almost gone from her little arms but still quite prominent on her thighs. I recon they too will have gone in about 2 weeks, have had Yvonne's sister Joyce visit and sat in the garden having a catch up on the past few weeks.

Wednesday was upon us before we knew it, Simon was due to arrive at 4 pm and today we had to do some shopping in Lowestoft. The last 24-48 hours have been quite hectic for some reason, washing some friends of Yvonne deciding to drop in for a cup of tea and a chat. It's annoying when you have a limited time constraint, how do you say to them "sorry but we have to go out." Naturally, we had to cancel doing some shopping till tomorrow, and as for the washing we were forced to delay it until they left at 2.40 pm. Simon arrived dead on time and removed a frame of some sort from the back of his van, "do you want some help?" I asked, "No that's fine!" he said. "I take it Amanda spends a lot of time sitting in her chair, laying on a type of airbed mat or sitting on your knees being cuddled am I correct?" he asked, "Amanda doesn't stand I take it?" "No!" I was rather annoyed him asking that as he could plainly see that with his own eyes. At this point he began fiddling with the piece of equipment he brought in, I'm not too sure he knew what he was doing as he was struggling unfortunately at one point trying to open it up. Eventually it appeared to be a type of crude wooden standing frame If I did not know any better it resembled a medieval stretching machine. 2 wide straps at the top to give some support to Amanda's back as she is standing, the top of the frame tucks under her arms and is slightly padded and a hinged wooden tray extended out the front. Just the look of it was not something of comfort, we strapped Amanda on it and it took less than a minute before she began crying. I removed her from it and told him to forget it, you can take it back with you when you go, but thanks for trying I think we need to look at something more practicable.

Clearly, we could never put Amanda through what can only be described as a torcher machine, she has suffered enough over the years I'm not going to allow her to suffer a contraption like that. Amanda remained restless for the rest of the day but glad to report she did not have any seizures; I might just put it down to a dreadful day as we all do at times. Amanda is going to have a day of excitement tomorrow as the school are taking her class swimming, I look forward to the results. Over the past seven weeks Amanda has been exceptionally well and had attended she apparently enjoys it immensely, after each session she becomes very relaxed school without missing a single day and as for her swimming trips well and supple exactly as she does after her baths at home.

Tomorrow as it is Sunday, and the weather forecast is that it will be dry and mild, we thought we would go to Sandringham Castle and on the way back stop off in Sheringham for something to eat before making our way home well at least that is the plan. We arrived at Sandringham just before 10.30 am and before doing anything else we had to have a drink, Amanda certainly was ready for liquid refreshment as well as her favourite Cherry Treat desert she loves it so much she will eat it at any time. With fed and watering completed we made our way to the main entrance of the castle grounds, what I did not expect was the long walk we had to face the other side of the main entrance. Disappointment set in when we eventually got to the Castle the royal family was not in residence, "Shame" never mind cannot have everything I suppose I will have to ring ahead next time and let them know we are coming. Well, we are one of their royal subjects after all are we not, I understand the little triangle sandwiches of cucumber egg and tuna are to die for only because you must eat so many to fill you up.

We had a guided tour through rooms in the Castle each one I lie to you not. The grandeur was completely and utterly mind blowing. It just shows you how the other half live, massive paintings hung on every wall of Princes Duke's Baronesses Lords and Ladies. Not even one was I think under six feet tall or if not taller and over five feet wide, thick red velvet looking curtains with white backing adorned every window which in themselves were ten or fifteen feet high. There were bookcases in a couple of rooms, one of which was floor to ceiling and full of books. I wonder how many have been read and who by, maybe I should ask the lady showing us round. Gold leaf I have never seen so much the figurines, ceiling decoration lights and coving covered in the stuff.

Time ran away from us, and it was a long walk back to the car. Amanda was getting crotchety, she needed changing and feeding. We were getting a little hungry to, firstly we must sort Amanda out. Luckly there is a café/restaurant on on the Castles grounds, we decided to use their changing facilities and at the same time get something to eat, unfortunately we were a little late for hot food, but they have sandwiches with various fillings. So, we purchased extortionately priced pre-packed sandwiches Ham and Cheese for Yvonne Egg mayonnaise and cress sandwiches for me tea and coffee, Cheese was like rubber and tasted like it too as for the egg well they had too much mayonnaise it literally squirted everywhere. I hasten to say we ended up not eating them, but the tea and coffee was not too bad.

Yvonne and I agreed that it was too late to stop off in Sheringham and decided we would make straight for home; we can do that another day when we have more time. Amanda bless her fell asleep in the car, and remained asleep till we got home. We were by then starving so stopped off to get some fish and chips from our local chippy, it has also started to rain but not hard. Amanda woke a little grumpy but after a night-time drink went off to sleep again, Amanda did not waken again till 7.15 am she was a little stiff but became quite supple after a hot bath.

Several weeks have past and Amanda has been exceptionally well, sleeping through the night eating drinking but more importantly not a single seizure. Hopefully, she will continue like this for as long as possible, even at school her teachers reports are encouragingly saying she is doing well. This will be good news to take back to the hospital clinic, along with the regular up to the minute graph charts I print out. Amanda received unbelievably a letter in the post this morning, which is the first time that has happened normally they address letters to me. I even check the envelope again just in case I made a mistake, but no, I did read it right "Ms. Amanda L Cherry" it was from the JP hospital informing her of her next appointment.

Yvonnes mum and dad came round and invited us round for Sunday Dinner, they have not had the opportunity to see us all for a couple of weeks and thought it would be nice to have us over. It is just passed 2.45 pm we were in the back garden soaking up some raise when the doorbell rang, it was our friend Kay she is a divorced mother with a disabled boy Jodie. When born he was starved of oxygen, but Kay brought him up on her own as his father Ray found he could not accept the disability. He is involved with taking him to hospital appointments and financially also allowing Kay time to do her own things by taking Jodie on days out, sadly she has medical issues herself suffering with severe migraine attacks.

Yvonne and I would visit them on a regular basis sometimes we would even stay for the weekend taking Amanda with us. We would often go swimming with Jodie and Amanda when the weather was suitable to do so, Yvonne had made friends with a woman called Diane who was going through a nasty family break up. She would allow us to use her swimming pool; If I am honest, I generally, feel it is in some way a bit of a trade-off. Yet while we were there, he seemed to be a nice person but on one occasion when we visited, Diane was really shaking and crying in the kitchen. Her husband Richard apparently went berserk smashing plates and cups, she told us that he had become angry because she was allowing us to use the pool.

Kay suggested that we do not use it anymore, but Diane was adamant that we do use the pool. We were invited as her friends and would not be intimidated by his bullying tack ticks, reluctantly we are not happy to use the pool if this was making her life at home difficult. Diane said please go to the pool and I will be out with some drinks and sandwiches, it was a little chilly even though the sun was shining so we did not stay in the pool too long and I do not think Jodie or Amanda were overly impressed by the looks on their faces.

Diane has made cheese and ham; egg and cress; tuna and cucumber and finally ham and pickle tea and coffee, clearly she had gone over the top a bit but with the tear wipped away and a smile on her face she helped to clear the food.

We had a wonderful day and thought it might be wise to say our thank you's and good byes before Richard made an appearance, it was rather uncomfortable for us leaving Diane alone but she asured us she would be fine. Sadly six weeks later I heard Diane could no longer tolerate the mental and at times physical abuse she moved out and got a flat. We have not seen her since, we pray things are good and that someday we will bump into each other and have a serious catch up.

Amanda has had some fantastic periods over the last few days, she has been having what we call mild seizures nothing violent needing hospital intervention. Nonetheless we still had to record them 172, we have received today in the post an appointment letter inviting us to attend doctor Patterson's clinic and also some blood test forms to check the drug levels before we attend. I don't mind saying this is one routine proceedure I detest most taking blood from Amanda, there has be occasions where to the annoyance of phlibotanists she would shut her veins down. I truly believe the same is felt by those taking the blood and are always apologising to us, but it is not us having the needles pushed into our bodies is it? Tomorrow we are taking Amanda to have her feet measured as we have seen some very pritty shoes in a sale, I'm hoping her feet are not too big it would be a shame not to be able to get them for her.

Well, we kind of overshot the new shoes for Amanda, they turned out to be too small. The shop assistant did say she would see if they could be ordered in, they would take about a week. "No thank you" said Yvonne I would have gone off them by then, it is rather a disappointing outcome but never mind we may find something else to take our fancy. As we left the shop who should we bump into but Kay and Jodie, "Hi there fancy meeting you here!" "Do you fancy a cuppa?" Yvonne asked "Yes why not" answered Kay. We made our way up to Chadds resturaunt, it is normally a little quiet at this time, and as they have a lift it is able to take the wheel chairs.

We were there for over an hour, almost and we had quite a chat. Kay invited us over next Friday to hers for the week-end. Jodie's school is having a fund raising day and she wondered if we would like to help with a stall, "I'm game if you are Yvonne" I said "without any hesitation why not!" she replied. The beauty of it all was how spontaniously quickly we responded, we had not asked what kind of stall Kay was running. It acctually turned out to be a burger stall, Yvonne was in the kitchen with Kay making tea's coffee's and soft drinks and I was cooking hot dog and burgers. Armed with a large pan of softened onions, four large boxes of 200 frozen burgers and 70 cheese slices. Sausages they were something else, 50 of the largest thickest sausages I have ever seen in my life all donated by a local butcher who was also a governor of the school.

I was blown away by the amount of people who attended my stall, some were returning time and time again. At one stage I almost ran out of onions panic set in and the kitchen staff crazyly chopped up more, and to get them soft the kitchen staff had to cook them on the gas oven. I must have cooked the hot dogs to perfection as they all went in one and a half hours, shortly after the onions ran out and finally the bread rolls. I was left with seven cooked burgers on the grill, and just under half a box of frozen bugers left in the fridge. I'll have to ask Kay later on how much made from the sale of the hot dogs and burgers, from the amount left over I recon we had a good day. Amanda and Jodie have been looked after by Janet and Faye Ward, I understand they have both been spoilt rotten by several families with ice cream and fruit juices. We may have a bit of a busy night ahead of us, lets pray that they have not been too greedy especially Amanda with her allagy to milk.

Our fears were proved quite fruitless both Jodie and Amanda were fine, infact both had the best nights sleep ever and remained asleep till ten fifteen this morning. Amanda Yvonne and me will be making our way home after tea tonight, we had a fantastic day yesturday and said we would like to do it again next time. Kay was unable to let me know how much I made on the burger stand, I was told the the money was totaled up all together when we finished and the total raised by every stall was £764.52p "not bad eh!" We eventually got home at 8.30pm, Amanda was sound asleep and; not wanting to wake her we put her straight to bed.

Yvonne and I were up early this morning, I had to make sure the schools reprt but was filled in and Amanda had some breakfast. Unfortunatley Amanda has had all her ready brek, so I thought I would make her some porrage oats in stead. It will be trial and error as she has not eaten it before, so hopefully she will enjoy it. Popped to the shop to purchase a couple of items including "Ready Brek" loaf of bread half dozen eggs and two pints of milk, postman braught us four pieces of mail and three were junk mail and a letter from the Hospital reminding us of Amanda's clinic appointment. For some reason I felt I needed to check my diary, it was a good thing as it turned out I had to have my car serviced at 3 pm today and had I not looked at the diary would have missed it. Nothing to worry about as the car was in good nick, I did get notified that I should consider over the next few months having my brake shoes changed as they were getting a little thin.

Wednesday arrived and the day began with rain and a little blustery, there was clear blue sky's heading from Beccles way hopefully reaching us before we had to leave for the hospital appointment. By the time we reached the hospital the rain had stopped and we were engulfed in warm sunshine, Amanda was fast asleep and believe it or not remained asleep even during her appointment. I was not expecting that as she was being pulled around quite a lot, Amanda stayed asleep until 7.30 pm we decided to give her a bath before teatime and that would save us from doing it in the morning.

Chapter Twenty-Five

A MAJOR OPPERATION

Well as I stated at the beginning of this book "Time passes all to quickly in this Life" and now Amanda has turned ten years of age, far greater than the two to eight estimation given by doctor Back and boy has she gone through so many traumatic and painful issues. In all that time Yvonne and I have found ourselves sitting on a knife's edge, wondering if this will be the time God decides to take her home. Let me be honest I have seen with my own eyes how close Amanda has had to be given resusitaion, we have continually and still do struggle with accepting doctor Backs diagnosis of Amanda's survial possibility. The many publicly verbal attacks I have made over the years regarding this man's so called integraty and ethicle beliefs, this has now taken away but are left with the emtional scars deeply burnt in our brains and heart.

Amanda has over the last few days been reasonably well, she has been having seizures still but they have been spasmodic and lasting for only seconds. It takes a trained eye to spot them, for an example we notice Amanda seems to be staring relentlessly into space. It is a strange feeling as you become aware that her eyes look glazed, then comes the twitching of arms and legs followed by a sound of grinding teeth but that is imposible as she had all her teeth removed several years back for health reasons. She then has a nack of holding her breathe only to then gasp when each seizure passes, small amounts of bubbly spital appear at both corners of of her mouth. The first time it happened was when Anne-Marie was in the front room shortly after we had just finished eating our tea, (bought in fish and chips). Yvonne and I were in the kitchen washing up suddenly Anne-Marie came running into the kitchen crying, "Mummy Amanda is not breathing and there are bubbles coming out of her mouth!" she cried. We could see the fear in Anne-Marie's face as the colour drained and she was quite shaken Like a shot Yvonne rushed hands dripping soap suds everywhere into the front room, grabing Amanda out of her chair laying her across her knees as one would do to a a child suffering from cystic fribosis. she began slapping heaverly on her back thinking that she was choking. We could see that Anne-Marie was so frightend as she ran to her bedroom sobbing, this was the first time she had seen this happen while on her own and clearly was enough to frighten both Yvonne and me even now.

Eventually things calmed down, it turned out that Amanda was having haing a seizure but not being in the room at the time we could not take any chances. The next task was to console Anne-Marie, Yvonne and I found this quite difficult as Anne-Marie convinced herself she had done something wrong and to cause the breathing problem. She was also angry that we had left her alone with Amanda while working in the kitchen, we certainly will not be doing that again in a hurry in future we will insure at least one of us will be in the room with Anne-Marie when she is left with Amanda.

We have noticed that Amanda has been over the last few weeks remaining rather rigid even after a daily steamy bath, as I mentioned sometime ago how relaxed Amanda now appears to last a little less each day. At preasent we are not too concerned and she is not showing any discomfort, I think it may just be a phase she is going through.

"Blooming heck!" I nearly forgot, Amanda has an appointment at the Victoria Road doctors surgery tomorrow. It do'es not happen that often the two clinic appointments would fall that close, "Silly Silly Me!" Would you believe it we arrived at the surgery 15 minutes before the appointment and eventually we were called 1 hour and 5minute's later, well by then Amanda had become really niffed and boy did she let the whole surgery know it. There was no way we could calm her, not being able to calm her down screaming flinging arms and legs was really embarrising at least it showed the staff members she had a strong set of lungs on her.

The examination took less than 20 minutes her wieght was good bloods and preasure satisfactory, there was some concern around sclorocis of her spine it maybe worth considering intervention of a made to measure gurdle to help prevent further twisting. The doctor said that he would refer her to a specialist, I wonder how long that will take. He also made a comment regarding the stiffness of her legs when checking hip joints, Amanda reacted quite strongly crying out loudly. It had been mentioned at her last hospital appointment and that the Clinicians there were concerned also, they may well revisit the problem as we have another appointment hospital this week.

Another long wait for Amanda to be seen, the hospital Clinic was packed so I had to stand as there were no empty seats available. Periodically the nurse receptionist would apologise for the delay in being seen due to the very large clinic attendance. Our polite response always is "that alright we are not going anywhere," when really I am thinking another long coffee break. Suddenly the examination room door would open, the anticipation of hearing Amanda's name being called is destroyed as a nurse exits the room. Then five minutes or so later again the door would open out comes the patient, the door closes again and another wait as they discuse the last patients examination findings. Eventually Amanda's name is called some ninety minutes after our appointed time slot.

As we expected the room was filled with several clinicians most of them we see on regular basis, but today sat in the corner of the room was a white haired gentleman we were told his name but regrettably I've forgotten it. His face was covered in wrinckles probably due to years of stress. Perched on the top of his head thin gold framed glasses which remained there throughout the entire clinic even while he was examining Amanda, it turns out that he had received a refural to have a look at the twist in Amanda's spine. He too had some concerns and verbally express them saying "This problem should have been addressed several years ago," he continued by saying "The twisting of her spine had most likely been caused by the huge number of grand-mal seizures over the years and to try and correct the problem may at this point be imposible.

The good news is he would like to hopefully try and prevent further spasticity by making a full body plastercast to wear, in turn it is somehow hoped to correct the pronounced curviture or at least reduce/slowdown the speed of the every increasing curviture. An urgent appointment would be arranged to see him again in his clinic where a cast can be made, "How long will Amanda have to wait for that appointment?" I asked. "1 weeks time and if you have not heard by then please phone my secretary and she will endevour to chase it up," he said. Dr. Patterson during his extensive examination spent a lengthy time talking to collegues unfortunately we were sat too far away to hear what they were discussing also to be fair he had his back to us. As usual I handed him my personal report on seizures and daily problems, he was pleased to read that while at home the seizures 84 in total since the last clinic were in many ways being controlled as is possible.

Doctor Patterson then raised the issue of the difficulty of Changing Amanda's nappy, she seemed to show a great deal of discomfort when nurses needed to change her. Although Yvonne and I were aware we realise now that it had become a problem, you some how believe it could be just a phase or it's just our imagination. Disbalief in our hearts that for months now we have both ignored the issue, the discomfort we have unintentionally put her through broke our hearts. "What can be done to remove the discomfort?" I asked, there was a short pause before he answered, he looked around at those in the room and then gently placed his pen down on the table. Since being made aware of the problem "I have spoken with some collegues, and a group consensous was reached to consider an invasive operation to remove a Femoral head from the top of either the left or right femor. In Amanda's case the right Femrol Head, clearly not something to rush into lightly. I asked "do you need an Answer now?" Doctor Patterson replied "No!" He would arrange another clinic appointment in about 3weeks time, by then MrVincent will have measured up and fitted her body Plastercast.

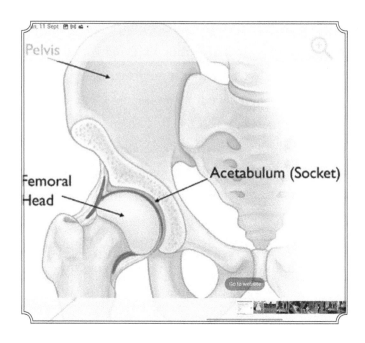

"That should give you hopefully time to make a decision one way or the other, "as you are well aware" he said. "Amanda will never be able to stand or walk on her legs, so there will never be an issue on that score and if we decided to go ahead it would certainly resolve any further discomfort she has with nappy changes or dressing." The downside to the operation is that Amanda's leg woulds in affect hang there doing nothing and would not allow her to stand on it should she ever reach that point.

The appointment has arrived today for the bodycast exactly 5 days after Amanda's clinic last week, it has been booked for 10.30am on Monday I hope there are no problems. The sun is shining and it is rather warm, the best news is we had no waiting room hanging about. We got to the waiting room sat down and within seconds Amanda was called, Yvonne went into the clinic with her and I waited in the waiting room. The proceedure took about 40 minutes to complete and now we have to wait for the body cast to dryout. The cast fitted just under Amanda's arms, ending roughly at her hips giving us the clearence to change nappies and such like. It looks quite hiddious and I mean seriously; seriously uncomfortable, Amanda certainly hated it as she was crying perfusly the whole time. Not only was it upsetting for Amanda but for us as well, another traumatic proceedure we were putting her through. Mr Vincent said "she will get use to it trust me," "how long will she need to wear this?" I asked. His reply was truly shocking "6 weeks and then I will see her in clinic to review how things have progressed." "Your having a laugh" I said, "6 weeks look at her she is clearly in distress what how is she going to be like 6 weeks from now?

It has been 3 days of sheer hell and stress for Amanda, she has really not slept since being in the cast. Amanda has not eaten but is taking fluid, but that is not a problem as we tube feed her. I am not sure just how much more she can take, it is clearly evident that placing Amanda in this cast is not working. She is so stressed out she has began having seizures, her body is over heating and we have purchased a desk fan that was a total waste of time and money, there is no way I am going to continue with this proceedure as it is in my opinion clearly an abuse matter. I am calling the Mr. Vincents clinic first thing tomorrow and demand that the cast be removed, Yvonne and I are at each other's throats over this to the point of emotional desperation constantly arguing the whole family are affected.

Last night was totally horendous I stayed up with Amanda in my arms on the couch, what with the seizures crying she finally managed to sleep no let me refraise that "cat napped" for about 5 five minute so if that. Saorse appeared under her arm and back of her neck, we endevoured to prevent them by creaming the back of her neck and under arms without success. The cast had to come off, we needed to seriously bring some urgent releif. With the cast removed the change in Amanda was instant, she became a different child no crying but still fitting our decicion to have the cast removed was I know the right one. Deep down in our hearts Amanda has suffered enough in her life now to have another painful proceedure forced upon her, the bodycast to help prevent further spinal deformaty was in hindsight clearly a step too far but nevertheless we took it and regreted it even to this day.

The actions of the passed few days have made us forget about the decission for the removal of Amanda's femeral head, I know what I have just said but I have been told the proceedure is fairly quick and as for the pain is controled by drugs for the first few days minimum. Anyway tomorrow we will have to really sit down and talk, this will be if we agree the biggest decision of our lives since Amanda was born. Do we go ahead with what is a major operation and would prevent her from walking on the leg, or do not go with it and possibly make the matter of her spine curveture mor pronounced due to the legs starting to cross? It is clearly a difficult decision to make, Yvonne and I took it to the rest of the family in hope they might make any decision may eventually make easier. How neive is that I ask, why would the family find it any easier than us.

Well the day of decision has arrived Amanda has her hospital appointment today at 2.30 pm, we have been battling with the realisation and the enormaty of putting Amanda through what will be a permanent life changing operation which may not work in her favour. Dr. Patterson apologised for the lengthy wait but his clinic was exceptionally large, he was taking a short break for 2 weeks and so needed to clear his clinic appointments before he left. I must admit he looked tierd and clearly was not his usual energetic self, he took the print out records I did at home as usual and had them placed in Amanda's hospital notes. He was dissapointed with the failure of the bodycast but he too thought it might not be a success either. Then he approached the matter of the surgery "have you thought anymore about Amanda's operation?" he said, "naturally I can't do anything till after my intended break."

I quickly looked over at Yvonne and squeezing her hand tightly turned to doctor Patterson and replied "YES!" "Even this three letter word prove to be a struggle to say we have, and would with some jeperdation like to go forward with the operation" we said. I think doctor Patterson picked up on a slight hesitency in our voices, what he din't know was that we still had that small issue of what if it goes wrong then what? "right" he said. "If you are both sure I will ask my secretary to look at a possible theatre date and we will book it in then we will see Amanda in say 3 weeks time.

True to his word an appointment to see doctor Patterson came through the letter box from the

James Paget Hospital, Amanda's clinic visit will be on Tuesday morning at 9.45 am. Naturally I would have to let the school know that she'll be not attending on Tuesday morning, Yvonne and I are out shpping so once we have finished on the way home we will call in and inform the class teacher. Typical english weather hit us while shopping in town, it hammered down with rain and the wind picked up so try to find shelter proved a bit of a problem as everyone had the same idea. One woman opened her umbrella only to have it turn insideout by the powerful wind, Yvonne and I made a dash for cover but gave up as we became absolutely drenched.

It rained for almost the whole week on and off, but today when we got up there was a change in the sky. The rain clouds covered the sky but surprise surprise just above the horizon the sky was beginning to light up with sunshine, "Wow!" what a beautiful sight to see things can only now get better. Well today wehave Amanda's hospital appointment and in someway we are more than a little apprehensive, well; why would we not be? as it was to discuss the proposed operation. As usual we arrived about 15 minutes early and even then the clinic was quite busy, I wonder how long we would be there before Amanda's name was called. We had bearly taken our seats when a voice called out

"Amanda Cherry!" "Well that is a first!" I said out loud, only to feel embarrassed the moment I said it, because the whole clinic had to go quiet as the word left my mouth.

Dr Patterson and his secretary were the only people in the room when we walked in, that in it's self was unexpected as normally there would be several clinicians from various departments with him. After welcoming us in he fliped through a couple of pages of Amanda's notes, then placing his pen down on the table in front of him asked us how Amanda has been since he last saw her. He knew about the problems with the bodycast and apologised for the distress it had caused, "How has she been seizure wise?" he asked. "No seisures at all" I replied "not a single one," He asked Yvonne if she would please lay Amanda on the examining couch while he conducts her vital signs. He listened to her chest and heart, manipulated her joints paying some attention to the moverability of her hip joints. "hum!" he said as Amanda reacted somewhat to that part of the examination by crying, but a few moments after she stopped. He felt all round her tummy and checked her eyes and finally looked in her ears, then walked back to his seat asking Yvonne to dress her again. Amanda has been eating well and sleeping better too, "Great!" he said "Great."

"Right Mr and Mrs Cherry you are both still happy that I carry out the oporation on Amanda's hip?" he asked, I could see that even as late as this Dr. Patterson knew we had some doubts. Nevertheless doubt or not we had been conviced that it was in Amanda's best interest to carry on with the oporation, so in unison we both replied "YES!" "Ok, I have booked the theatre for next Wednesday week at 3.50 pm, I would like to have Amanda admitted early on Tuesday morning for post op checks." Nerves began to raise our emotions as we thought it would happen this quickly, really I recon we would feel the same if it were planned to happen next month or tomorrow.

Yvonne and I were up with the lark, after giving Amanda a bath and dressed her she devoured a bowl of Ready Brek infact, I don't think it even touched the sides if I am truely honest. Even her milky tea went down so fast you'd think she was in a hurry to go somewhere, it was somewhat chilly outside so on with a coat gloves scarf and fur lined boots we set of for the hospital. It was quite windy and was beginning to rain, fortunately the rain did not last and by the time we got to the hospital the clouds had past but there was still quite a cold nip in the air.

We arrived on the childrens ward at 9.15 am, this seemed to be Amanda's first home as she has spent more time here than at home. Obsovations carried out, booking in done wrist bands attached to her arm and left leg, we were left with our thoughts. Doctor Patterson or one of his interns were not due to appear until 4.30 pm, the staff kept us going with cups of tea and coffee and at dinner time we went down to the restaurant for a meal. My favourite Steak and Kidney Pie chips peas and thick gravy Yvonne would have Chicken mash potato vegetables and gravy, that would keep us satisfied till we got home at least.Amanda spent most of the day asleep, and only woke up when the nurses came and did their observations. Naturally when doctor Patterson and his team arrived it was seriously a much different kettle of fish, again he pulled twisted and splade her thighs simular to the test you might give a child to see if there was an displacement of hip joint and pelvis. It was clear this was painful for Amanda as she screemed out just as she did in his clinic, mind you he seemed to perform the proceedure with a great deal more vigor than before.

With his examination complete they left the room and stood round the nurses station, "what do you call a group of doctors in a huddle?" I asked myself. "Flock of sheep, Gaggle of Geese," but for Doctors I find it very mistifying to say the least. Anyway they finished discussing things as Dr. Pattersons bleeper went off, one of his interns came into the room apologised for the delay and informed us that Mr. Patterson has booked the theatre for 10 am tomorrow to carry out Amanda's femoral head removal proceedure. "Well darling we have now committed ourselves and there is no turning back" I said, Yvonne gripped my hand and smiled as we both glanced at Amanda laying in her cot.

Amanda was asleep when we left for home, events planned for tomorrow high on our minds as we drove away from the hospital. Even now that nagging feeling of intrepodation on what was about to happen, Amanda was going to theatre at 10 am so we decided to go to see her at 12 pm she should be out of surgery and back on the ward by then. Nothing in this life works as planned so why should today be any exception, we arrived on the ward to find that Amanda has not been brought back from the recovery room. Sandra Mills the duty ward sister explained that unfortunately after surgery Amanda had 3 quite large seizures and could not send her back, doctor patterson will explain more when he comes up to do his rounds.

Amanda returned shortly after 1.30 pm, she appeared quite pale and had been sedated. Doctor Patterson came to let us know that the surgery had been very successful, it was while in recovery she presented a major gran-mal seizure which lasted for 15 minutes followed by 2 more. They naturally had to visually monitor her closely until she stopped fitting, they had to give her 10 mg of rectal valium so that's is why she is how she is. I asked about the reason for her right leg being heavily bandaged and held in traction with weights and a pullyat the end of her cot. (*Diagram below is for demonstration use only.*)

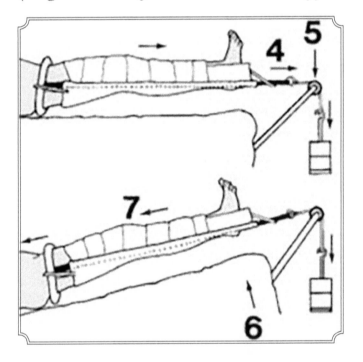

Basically "Amanda has as you know had the femoral head removed from the femor, so while the wound heals the bandages help keep her leg fixed and comfortly supported which inturn assists in reducing muscule shrinkage." He explained He went on to say "this whole proceedure also greatly reduces any pain while weights on the frame keeps the to of the fermour from rubbing against the socket."

"How long will she be trust up like this?" I asked "about 6 - 8 weeks inicially" he said, "depending on the speed of healing I will then re-assess her then decide on the next move" he replied. "Well, Amanda remained in hospital for 2 weeks and has I am pleased to report tolerated all the bandages weighted legs and pain killers since the operation." Doctor Patterson has visited Amanda this morning before we arrived acording to the sister he is very pleased with her progress, she informed us he would call on the ward later to speak to us. Again true to his word doctor Patterson came and saw us, "Good afternoon Mr. and Mrs Cherry!" "How do you find Amanda today?" he asked. "very good" I said "to be fair she has been like this for quite a few days I'm pleased to say."

"Well how would you feel about taking her home tomorrow?" "I am happy for you to take her as you are capable in continuing with her care at home" he said. This was the best news of the day, although we were concerned this morning on why he wanted to speak with us and now we know.

Chapter Twenty-Six

GOODNIGHT SWEETHEART GOODNIGHT

"No way were we going to be late getting to the hospital this morning," the excitement of getting Amanda home is overwhelmingly strong. As everyone knows we are the same every time Amanda comes out of hospital, the fear and trepedation when she goes into hospital is mentally distressing for everyone in the family. From our experience those members of staff who have known Amanda over the years go through the same stressfull emotions, I know nursing staff hate becoming attatched to their patients but in many many cases such as with Amanda it does happen. The excitement in getting Amanda home is always frustatingly mared by the hospital farmacy, doctors discharge papers signed and medical care packages arranged everything is stopped because of delays by the chemist department.

Eventually some 30 minutes later her medication finds its way on to the ward and we are off, first port of call is to Victoria Road Surgery to hand over Amanda's discharge letter. One less job to do and the fact we had to pass the surgery on the way to get home anyway, Amanda slept all the way home as normal I think it is the motion of the car and hum of its engine that knocks her out. Leaving there we traveled to Yvonne's mum and dad boy were they pleased to see her, out came the best china cups dad made the tea and coffee just to keep us there so everyone could give her some cuddles. Not an easy job as her leg was strapped up with bandages, something we will have to get use to for the near future.

It was 5.30 pm when we finally walked through our front door, we were absolutly starving "who's for fish and chips?" I said. "That is a good call dad" said Anne-marie, "great while I go and get them can you help mum with Amanda's tea and after tea I'll sort out Amanda's bed with the pully system." That was the best Fish and Chips I tasted in sometime, Anne-marie sadly found a large fishbone in her meal she made such fuss I said to her "your lucky you found it you might have swallowed it and got stuck darling."

For the next 3 weeks at 10.15 am we had a regular visit from a nurse, she would change Amanda's bandage once a week and wash Amanda's wound every other day. She would leave the wound open to the air for about 30 minutes, the sight of the scar was not a pleasant sight it was about 3-4 inches in length and quite sore looking. Really it was a neat looking scar flat lying no ugly ridge, clearly a well performed proceedure and not a bodge up job. We made Amand jelly and ice cream for dinner, after a couple of mouthfulls Amanda decided to sneeze as I was putting the spoon into her mouth, yes you guessed it went everywhere mainly over me though. Her chair, the walls the carpet you name it Yvonne and Anne-marie burst into hystericle and uncontrolable laughter. That will certainly be one for the book, especially as I did not have to clean it up Yvonne took the task on. Blimmy it even reach the TV screen,

Well it has been almost 4 weeks since Amanda had the operation and she has heald fantastically, stitches have been removed and the bandage has come off. Amanda can now be given a bath and nolonger do'es she need to be attatched to the weight pully frame at night, we have had a couple of days where Amanda has not respnded well to the weights but is now ok. She has not returned to school yet, I feel she would really benefit from I think another 2-3 weeks but will discuss it with doctor Patterson at her next clinic appointment in 5 days time.

Anne-marie asked if she could take her Sister out for a walk to the Nicholas Everett park which is about a mile away from us, Yvonne and I were hesitent at first as we recall the last episode when she was left alone with her sister. I will not be alone mum Karren will be with me, "Ok" Yvonne said but I want you back here in about the next 2 hours or earlier if needed. Anne-marie's eyes lit up and said "Yessssss!" I am douptful she will be gone too long as I can see some really black storm clouds were heading our way us from the Beccles direction, sure enough the wind increesed and half an hour after leaving home Anne-marie Amanda and Karren waled in the door. Anne-marie said "the wind picked up it was really cold and we did'nt want to get caught in the rain," it was a very sencible call made by the girls as 20 minutes later the heavens opened and the driving rain hit hard.

It rained heavenly for over an hour, so much water almost flooded the front door not even the storm drain could handle the flow. I was so concerned I offered to drive Karren home just in case it started again, pleased to say it brightened up and we took Karren home in the car anyway. We have allowed

Anne-marie to take Amanda out for walks on may occasions since, she is proving to be a real asset lately and the fear of passed episodes have gone completely and to say she is excited when she takes Amanda out is a real understament of the fact.

It has been almost 17 weeks since Amanda had the operation and clearly her state of health has been fantastic especially concerning her seizures, but this morning Amanda was not as happy as she had been over the past few weeks. "What were we about to see?" Amanda has become avery irritable child all of a sudden, we are unable to put a finger on the reasons why. Maybe she was coming down with something I understand there have been several children who have been kept off school due to illness, Amanda is very supseptable to catching bugs and such like the school keeps us up to date with any problems that may arise. So we have kept Amanda home until we are given the all clear, the withdrawl of Amanda from school lasted just over 3 weeks and the school informed us that whatever it was has now cleared.

The bug or whatever it was may have gone from the school but Amanda we still the same, while off school it became quite evident that the problem was eminating from Amanda's hip as everytime she was physically moved / picked up sat down or placed on the floor she would start crying. While changing her we also began to notice that her hip would make a clunking noise and she again would start crying, we made an appointment to see her GP and believes that it is mother nature creating the problem. "feel this is due to the fact Amanda is still growing and what mother nature is doing is growing a new piece of bone and unfortunately is catching her femeral ball socket." he said. "Amanda will need to be put back into tempory tracktion and prescribed some pain cover, it was really not the recommendation I was looking for but it is what it is. With Amanda back in traction she became a little settled, it was mainly changing her nappies that created the problem she was having and the pain. No one likes seeing someone in any sort of discomfort, Yvonne and I were no different but we have over the years learnt not to panic too much and to allow any much needed intervention to be the final straw.

Chapter Twenty-Seven

THE FINAL CHAPTER

Amanda remained in traction for just under 2 weeks, really it was to prove fruitless she became very sensitive to the slightest movement and would litterally screem out and as for the clicking hip syndrome it was quite noticable and loud. We clearly were struggling with Amanda's crying I telephoned the childrens ward, a sister Mason eventually answered the phone, I explained who I was and the reason for my call. "Can I bring Amanda in to have a doctor to look at her," I asked "Amanda is in so much pain nothing I do seems to be helping and as you can hear she is screeming in pain." There was a slight pause before she spoke, "Yes by all means Mr Cherry you can bring her in but she will have to admitted."

I had no other choice but to agree and told her we would be there in about 20 minutes or so, everything and I mean everything was out to try and prevent us getting to the hospital. Victoria Road railway crossing's gates were down for just under 4 minute wait; then would you believe the oulton broad lock gates opening took another 5 minutes. If that was not enough we were stopped by a zebra crossing and Oulton Broad North Railway crossing, that's a first and I am certain I could ever do that again even if I tried. The nurses were on the ball when we arrived, Amanda was admitted and half an hour later the duty doctor arrived to examin her. As usual this part is the boring part as one has to explain what has gone on since last admitted and takes the longest time, we were offered a cup of tea and coffee while the protacols are carried out and is to be fair a real welcome.

With our 19th Wedding anniversary on Monday coming, I had to ask the question "how long will Amanda have to stay in hospital?" I agree it was really a selfish question to ask, we should really be thinking of Amanda and her health needs not worrying about anniversaries and things. "I think it will be about a couple of weeks, or until we are at least able to sort something out with Amanda's leg." he said. It was disapointing as we had arrange a family bash to celebrate 19 years of marage, but more poinient everyone predicted it would not last 6 months how wrong can people be "eh!" Never mind we will celebrate it later when Amanda is home again, examination over and Amanda tucked up in bed it was time to give Amanda her medication and something to eat.

What we did'nt know that waiting in the wings was the hospital pathologist ready to pounce on Amanda, the act of taking blood from her was unpleasent at the best of times so we would always leave the room and get a tea/coffee. Amanda was never keen on it either but it had to be done at some point, with the proceedure done she was still crying when we got back Yvonne unhooked her from the weights and cuddled her till she fell asleep. Amanda was also hooked Up to an IV as the doctor felt she was a little dehydrated, Yvonne and I were not surprised by that as whenever she is admitted that is a normal proceedure. We left for home at 9.30 pm and as we were tiered exhausted and very hungry, the one problem we both had was we had no food in the house and would have to do an urgent shop first thing tomorrow.

It is clearly not advisable to sleep on an empty stomach, as we both had a very disturbed night. Gurgling noises along with stomach cramps did not help, we did our shop and made some breakfast at home before going to the hospital to see Amanda Anne – marie came with us and as usual she was excited. Now a teenager she enjoyed looking after her sister and visiting her when she was hospitalised, as parents Yvonne and I were worried about any resentment she might have built up over the years; resentment possibly for being push to one side. Lets face it since Amanda was born life quickly changed the family make up, Anne – marie spent a great deal of her childhood being braught up by Yvonne's mum and dad something we both regret every single day and feel deeply guilty about.

Yvonne and I have tried so many times to have family chats but without success, something would always get in the way preventing us from talking about problems worries or anger issues. Eventually by sheer chance Anne-marie and Yvonne were in the kitchen together, when the subject of Amanda came into the conversation. Anne-marie asked "now that Amanda has had this operation on her leg will she ever be able to stand?" Clearly this question was Was an easy one to answer, unintentionaly it opened up a chance to ask about how she felt about the way we have handled things in general. Did she feel any anger or jealousy twoward us or her Sister, explaining that over the years our lives have been centred mainly on Amanda and inadvertantly that had a serious effect on us bringing you up. "Your Dad and I feel guilty/ashamed and yes angry with ourselves for not being there for you!"

Yvonne was quite surprised at the response Anne-marie came back with, "Amanda is my little sister a sister who has an illness and needs more attention than me! and anyway mum," she said "It has been very difficult for you and dad and "I know you love me as much as my sister but she needs a lot more than me." Yvonne cuddled Anne-marie tightly as a tear ran down her cheek, when I heard this the feeling of shame struck hard. We have been so tied up with Amanda's problems, we had sadly lost that close family bond I thought we had somewhere along the way. Thinking back on it now I wonder if it could have been the start when Anne-marie was found crying in her bedroom by her mum, when asked what was wrong? she said "I think I'm pregnant mum and I'm so frightend to tell you and dad." Taking her hand Yvonne said "come on We'll both go and tell your dad."

I was watching "Sparticus" on Video when the door opened and Yvonne walked in, Anne-marie had her head bowed and was sobbing. I knew that something was obviously wrong, then Yvonne said "Anne-marie has something to tell you." Clearly

Anne-marie was seriously upset about something not only was she sobbing but she was also noticably shaking. When she told me I remember just sitting there really not believing we were going to be a grand parents, Naturally I can't say I was not disapointed on hearing the news but I was. The strange thing was I felt no anger quite the oposite in fact, it certainly was far too late to ramp and rage. I'm quite sure Anne-marie was taken a-back by the way I reacted, but what could I do "well my darling it takes two" I said I flung my arms around her gave her a really big hug; congratulated both her and her boyfriend Denise on the pregnacy but more importantly assured them of our support for the future.

Amanda has been in hospital two days now, when we arrived on Wednesday morning there was clearly a different atmophere on the ward. Something was not as relaxing as normal, there was an air of worry about the nursing staff no happy jovial chatting or a welcoming smile as we entered the ward. It was not until much later in the day that one of the nurses let slip that several patients had come down with a sickness bug and it was getting worse, "why were we not told till now?" I have braught Amanda onto a hospital ward that has a rampent viral infection placing Amanda in danger of catching it, I am so angry they know Amanda's immunity system is very poor and that she picks things up very easily. Nothing but nothing was going to prevent me from raising this matter with the hospital administration department and with doctor Patterson, in my opinion this is confirming my fears on how incomputent the hospitals so called administration is.

Over the next couple of days Amanda failed to improve, this infection was highly toxic the medical staff were struggling to irradicate it from the ward completely. I say the ward because to our knowledge it was at this time only centered within the childrens ward, and boy were the nurses looking worn out they clearly were almost trapped within the department for their whole 12 -13 hour shift. However upsetting it was for us as parents, it was certainly was clear to us the stress placed on the medical staff. Yvonne and I tried to ease the workload by administating her feeds and drugs, this freed up nurses to look after other patients. But then we have assisted like that everytime Amanda was admitted to hospital, at this time I was aware that other parents had the same idea and were doing the same. I'm sure the pressure for at least two of the nurses became too much, (they were both trainee and had been sacconded from another department) as they appeared quite upset at the nurses station.

Sunday morning arrived in all its glory, wet cold and windy not at all friendly. We decided to have something to eat at the hospital so skipped breakfast, which on occasions we do and will go early so we are able to also have a drink as well. We arrived at 9.30 am and after Sausage 2 egg, bacon hashbrown and beans we were both set up for the problems of the day to come. There was no real change on the ward the day shift were just as busy working as normal, but as we walked in to Amanda's room a nurse had just replaced Amanda's NG tube and she was about to give her a drink. As usual I picked up her record sheets which I find an enormous amount of information regarding what has been going on while we are at home etc, I know it is wrong of me to do this but I have always done it.

Today of all days I wish I had not read them, Amanda had not been well through the night and has been quite sick. They have been giving her 200mls of clear water every two hours, her sickness (vomiting) seems to have subsided for now but she has become very sleepy. A duty doctor regularaly entered her room and kept checking her over quite mathodically, I asked the doctor; why was she closely monitoring her. She told me Amanda was worrying them and confirmed she had caught the infection going round the ward, because she was volnerable they needed to keep a close eye on her for the time being. If nothing else I have learnt over the years, if doctors say they are worried or even concerned about Amanda's health then that worry and concern also rub off on me.

As Sunday progressed I counted 18 visits from doctors the 200mls of water Continued none stop every 2 hours, and Yvonne and I were giving her the drinks as well. I raised my conserns with the Staff nurse, all this fluid you are giving her she has at no time has she been to the loo, surely that is wrong her nappy remains totally dry. Doctors seemed to be unconcerned explaining they will continue to monitor the issue, I was not having that and I was seriously becoming more and more angry as more and more they refused to listen to my concerns. Time and time again I asked doctors and nurses about where is the fluid going and why is she not weeing, I found myself once more fighting to be urgently listend too. Clearly I was fighting a losing battle, why oh why were they ignoring me, I was so concernd and upset tears were rolling down my face. Eventually they sent a hospital social worker to have a word, we are scared that something major was wrong with Amanda. "All day to day Amanda has been given 200mls of clear water every two hours, and yet she has not been to the loo once." I said.

Even that compliant to the social worker fell on deaf ears, we were worried that something was wrong with her kidney's. "Had she got an infection and that was the reason she has not passed any urine? " I said, "we really don't know" or clearly; was there a much more serious problem doctors have missed. I sat holding Amanda's hand with my chin resting on the on the edge of her bed, I was so close to her face I could feel her breath on my nose. It sounded a little laboured but I put that down to whatever infection she had caught, massaging her tiny hands with my thumb and gently stroking her head which must have had a calming effect. Her eyes were closed and she had what appeared to be a smile on her face, she looked so beautiful and peaceful as she lay there.

How quickly things can change, Amanda suddenly stoped beathing for a few seconds then started again. I took no notice of it at first but then she did it again, I rushed to the door and called out loudly for help as I turned back to Amanda she seemed for a second to choke. Suddenly she had water gushing out of her mouth nose ears and eyes, as I grabbed her in my arms the nurse entered saw what was happening and pulled the emergency alarm switch. Amanda was taken from me and Yvonne and I were removed from the room, the speed in which the hospital medical crash team arrived in the room sometime later suggested they were expecting this emergency to happen. Yvonne and I were as you might expect beside ourselves, we were screaming out for someone to let us know what was happing.

Looking into the room from outside another hospital room Amanda was surounded by at least two doctors and 5 nurses, both Yvonne and I were shacking and crying but with all those bodies around her we were unable to see what was going on. Yvonne and I were holding each other tightly and praying Amanda would be "OK," I think they were working on her for well over 10 minutes or so. Our brains were working overtime it was not good and as we watched members of staff one by one leave the room, we were approach by staff nurse Kelly Summers and a Doctor Blake their heads were hung low. "we are so so sorry Mr and Mrs Cherry!" we were unable to save Amanda" they said, Yvonne ran back in the room and I totally lost it my emotions took on a life of their own yelling blaming everyone; punching and kicking the wards central pillars over turning a table. It has happened our worst nightmares have come home to roost albeit some 8 yrs later.

When all the anger and physical emotional venting had finished, I realised I was not the only person greiving I was rejoined by Staff nurse Summers with her arms around Yvonne shoulders. It must be very difficult for hospital staff to deal with the loss of any child on their watch, but more so I guess with Amanda a regular patient in their care. Who consoles them in needy times as they are trying to console now, we just wanted to get back to being with Amanda she is on her own. We both were trying to resist being taken to the parents room, staff nurse Summers explaining that they needed to sort Amanda out and we could go back to her shortly. Two young nurses appeared with hot drinks and plenty of sugar, our strength has been serverely reduced and it was important that we keep that up.

Hot sugary drinks were the last thing on our minds, we just wanted to get back to Amanda. "What was taking them so long?" I could feel the frustration in me building up inside voices constantly saying, Amanda needs you both over and over and over again. The pain is so strong I am finding it difficult to beathe, I was clinging on to Yvonne's hands so tightly I must have stopped her blood circulation I know my knuckles were turning white. Eventually what seemed Like hours later we were allowed back in Amanda's room, we again filled up with tears as the nursing staff had dressed her in a white nighty removed the NG tube from her nose leaving a redish mark where the plaster had been brushed her hair and replaced the bed linin. The pillows had been removed and placed in her hands a small light brown bear, she looked so beautifull laying there and if I did not know any better it was like she was asleep. They had even dimmed down the light in the room, as we watched her lifeless body for a moment laying there I swear I could see her chest raise and fall albeit slowly.

The need to hold her in our arms again just one more time was so strong I rolled back the bed clothes and gently lifted her up to give her to Yvonne to cuddle I heard what sounded like a breath being taken, the nurse informed me that this was quite natural as air sometimes become lodged just like wind and is expelled when the body is moved. As I got my last cuddle the issue of blame for what had happened began to take hold, it was impossible to blame anyone but myself. "I have said this earlier the only person who can be blamed for Amanda's demise I caused the death of my daughter if I had not been so keen in getting her into hospital she would still be with us alive. I hate myself and will Always do so, I'm not able to ask Amanda for her forgiveness it was beginning to eat away at me more and more the more I thought about it the worse it got.

I did not tell Yvonne or any other family member how emotionally angry I had become with myself, Yvonne and I reluctantly and tearfully left for home at 10 pm. We had to let the family know that Amanda had passed away. It was not going to be easy telling Anne-marie and were dreading it, should we tell her or should we ask Yvonne's mum and dad to do the telling. Really it was a no brainer as parents we need to tell her that her sister had died, and we both were Not looking forward to tell her or other family members. I think Mum and Dad had senced that something had happened when we walked into the house, mum grabed Yvonne in her arms for what seemed like hours both crying and as for dad he slumped down on a chair and bowed his head crying. It was what happened next that hit us hard Anne-marie came into the dinning room saw everyone in tears, "whats happened dad why is everyone crying?" she asked. I struggled to find the courage to say "your sister has gone, she's died darling."

Anne-marie screamed and crying as she ran to her mum throwing her arms around her she was unconsoleable, the hard part was not knowing where to go next. There was still the issue of telling the rest of the family both here in Lowestoft and further afield, mum instintavly took the bull by the horns "I will let everyone know in the morning it too late to contact them now." She said. You both looked really shattered, Anne-marie can stay with us if she liked. "No nanny" she said, "I want to go home with mum and dad." Anne-marie slept with her mum, my mind was desperately trying to proccess all what has happened still blaming myself failing to understand just why I am not being punished.

I spent about an hour or so I think just staring at the ceiling I was aware of Anne-marie crying just showed how thin the walls were, I went into the Kitchen and made a cup of coffee no idea how many sugars I spooned into the mug but I think it was quite sweet. I spent much of the night going over photograph's, I must have fallen asleep around 2 am I awoke startled at 3.40 am when the Photograph Album hit the floor along with the coffee mug. Luckly I had finished the coffee before I dropped of to sleep, The bungalow was eireyly silent Anne-marie must have finally cried herself to sleep. Sandra Bullen a health social worker arrived at our front door it was 10.30am, she had come to help us with sorting out Death certificates; registration of death and funeral directors.

There is quite a lot of organising form filling notifying departments of Amanda's passing including the council housing department, Amanda has only been gone less than 24 hours and they wanted us out of the bungalow by the end of the week. How callious now is that, "well I tell you now for nothing that ain't going to happen anytime soon," I told the housing officer. "This bungalow has now become a shrine real deep memories of Amanda are deeply embeded into the walls and I will only leave when I decide, not by you!" I angrily said. "I am still paying my rent so how dare you try and push us out before I am ready, "Mr. Cherry, we have a family in urgent need of this property pease when would you be ready to move?" he asked.

What I did not inform him of was Yvonne and I knew the family he was talking about, a family who we became close to and visited many times in a month through the disable club in Lowestoft. Infact we had been talking with them about eventually moving, and although they were eager to move in they told us that we should not go until we were ready. Six weeks after Amanda's funeral our lives took direction, a close and valid friend of Yvonne's telephoned to inform us of a house that had just come up on the market. It was actually just across the road from them in

Hardy Close it was empty and would we pop over to have a look, at first we did not want to leave the bungalow but then saw no reason why we should not at least take a look. We approached the estate agents and ask if we could look round the property with the intention of purchasinig it, the front and back garden needed some tiedying up but when we entered the property "WOW!" We fell in love with it. I explained that Waveney District Council Housing would be purchasing it on our behalf, before I had even told them we found a property. We made an appointment with the housing officer the same day, I asked the Housing Officer how urgently did he want us to vacate the bungalow "As soon as posible." He said. I told him we had found a property but it was privately owned and we would be willing to move if the Council would concider buying it.

I have never seen the Councel move so fast, it took them exactly 3 weeks to finalise the purchase. I was also promised all our moving costs would be covered by the Council, so they were genuine in getting us out as quickly as possible, we moved out.

"Finally"

Life is like an open book with many chapters and many open doors, eventually you find yourself faced with that last concluding chapter and a final door to close. No easy thing to face for anyone, but face it we must as we begin to create new chapters in our lives as we move on. (past memories are stored in our hearts and will never be forgotten)….. **"God Bless you Amanda till we meet again" " WE MISS YOU DEEPLY and LOVE YOU MORE" THE END!**

Unequivocal Love
A True Story

By
Malcolm Cherry

"GRIEF"

IT IS AN EMOTIONAL EXPERIENCE MOST OF US WILL AT SOME POINT IN OUR LIVES FACE, AT THE LOWEST TIME OF YOUR LIFE A WELL-MEANING MEMBER OF SOCIETY TRIES TO CONVINCE YOU THAT THOSE FEELINGS OF LOSS YOU ARE EXPERIENCING WILL GIVEN TIME GET BETTER. "STOP RIGHT THERE, IT DON'T!"

"For me;" the last 33 years have just flown by, as parents of a severely disabled child Yvonne and I have been trapped in a world of tears, joy, laughter, and grief. The emotional pain one feels when a child, your child dies crushes your very being. The anger rushing through my body is ripping us apart, ultimately, I blame myself for her death. By insisting she be admitted into hospital she would have been safe at home, and clearly would not have caught the rampant viral infection on the ward. There are still far too many un-answered questions that now will remain so, I made a promise 33 years ago to Amanda that I will I write her story and if possible have it published. I'd like parents who have found themselves in the same grief struggling battle, find some way comfort from the fact they are not alone.

"We have been there; "No!"
correction! we are Still there."

Malcolm Cherry (2023)

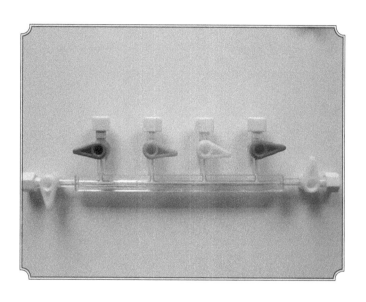